EXPLORE
SINGAPORE

CONTENTS

Introduction

Directory

Credits

Best Routes

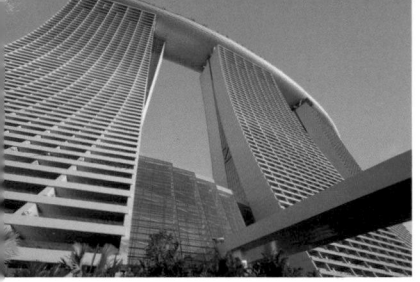

ARCHITECTURE

Don't miss grand colonial-era buildings in the Civic District (route 1), skyscrapers designed by superstar architects in Marina Bay (route 3), or flamboyant Peranakan terrace houses in Emerald Hill (route 7).

RECOMMENDED ROUTES FOR...

THE ARTS

Take in a music or theatre performance at The Esplanade – Theatres on the Bay (route 3), spot public sculptures in the CBD (route 5), and sample Southeast Asian art in the Singapore Art Museum (route 2).

FOODIES

Food-lovers won't be disappointed with the Singapore-style seafood in the East Coast (route 15) and the hawker offerings at Maxwell Road Food Centre and Chinatown Food Street (route 6).

LOCAL CULTURE

Explore the city's eclectic cultures in its ethnic neighbourhoods (routes 6 and 9). For a glimpse into the Straits Chinese way of life, wander around Katong (route 15) or visit the Peranakan Museum (route 2).

NIGHTLIFE

Flashy clubs at Clarke Quay (route 4) and Marina Bay Sands (route 3) are great for all-night partying. Sentosa (route 11) has laid-back beach bars and jazz fans should head to Bali Lane at Kampong Glam (route 9).

PARKS AND GARDENS

Opt for a leisurely walk in Gardens by the Bay (route 3) or wander in the landscaped Botanic Gardens, before checking out gorgeous orchids in the National Orchid Garden (route 8).

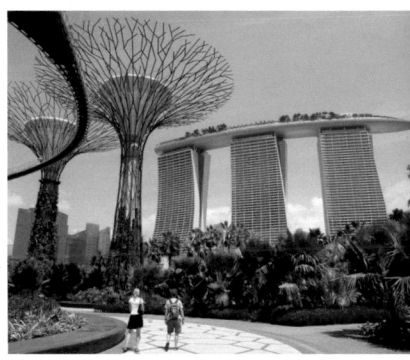

SHOPAHOLICS

Mall-hop on Orchard Road (route 7), browse idiosyncratic shops in Kampong Glam (route 9), comb Chinatown (route 6) and Little India (route 10) for cultural finds, and splurge at VivoCity (route 14).

WILDLIFE

The city's animal parks impress with their naturalistic habitats and conservation focus. Set aside a day for the Singapore Zoo, River Safari and Night Safari (route 18) and make a trip to the Jurong BirdPark (route 13).

INTRODUCTION

An introduction to Singapore's geography, customs and culture, plus illuminating background information on cuisine, history and what to do when you're there.

Chinatown's night market from above

EXPLORE SINGAPORE

The small city-island state of Singapore has achieved much and has even grander ambitions, but its most distinct joys are found in its warm, eclectic people, ethnic neighbourhoods, and the pleasure of food, shopping and nightlife.

For some, Singapore is merely a welcome stopover, its top-rated airport making it the perfect gateway to Southeast Asia. For others, this tiny island, with its legendary cleanliness, widespread use of English as well as celebrated sights, shops, eateries and colourful ethnic neighbourhoods, is an appealing destination in its own right; an ideal introduction, in fact, to all of Asia in one fell swoop.

DEVELOPMENT

In 1819, Englishman Thomas Stamford Raffles from the British East India Company founded modern Singapore. Recognising the potential of this tiny blip of an island shrouded in jungle and swamp and occupied only by Orang Laut (Sea People), a few Malay families and some Chinese traders, he went on to set up a trading post. He ordered the land to be cleared, supervised an ambitious construction campaign, and welcomed labourers and merchants from China, India and all over Southeast Asia. His free-trade policies soon created a boomtown of 10,000 residents, at which

some 2,000 ships called annually. In short, Raffles laid the groundwork for the vibrant free port of Singapore that remains in place today.

Modern-day Singapore

Singapore's modern-day visionary was Lee Kuan Yew, the first prime minister. Under the direction of Lee and his successors, Goh Chok Tong and Lee Hsien Loong, Singapore has continued to be one of Southeast Asia's brightest stars over the past four decades. The government's paternal approach has defused racial and labour disputes, its public housing schemes have provided most citizens with their own homes, and its savvy economic policies have attracted foreign trade and investment.

Its invasive socialengineering policies – from banning smoking in public places and outlawing the sale of chewing gum, to monitoring flushing in public toilets and imposing huge taxes on car ownership – may have drawn sneers from the Western media, but Singapore is undeniably the cleanest and most orderly of all Asian cities. What some Westerners perceive

The Raffles statue   *At a Grand Prix concert*

as draconian laws and little personal freedom in an authoritarian state, are regarded by many pragmatic Singaporeans as merely the common-sense way to run a country. For an insight into Singapore's meteoric rise, read *The Singapore Story*, the vivid and fascinating memoirs of Lee Kuan Yew, who, whether you like him or not, has been credited with guiding the country to where it is today.

ORIENTATION

Located at the southern tip of peninsular Malaysia, Singapore consists of the main island, which is 699 sq km (270 sq miles) in area, and 63 other smaller islands. Most of the main island is less than 15m (50ft) above sea level, and the highest point is Bukit Timah Hill, at 163.63m (537ft).

Downtown Singapore remains largely arranged according to the original town plans Raffles had executed in 1819. The colonial hub of the city, today's Civic District, is still the heart of the administration, as it was in Raffles' time. The clamour of Chinatown and the hum of business in the Central Business District around Raffles Place have not diminished. The Muslim area of Kampong Glam and the predominantly Hindu Little India retain their ethnic feel. Chic Orchard Road, a plantation area in colonial times, has been transformed into one of Asia's premier shopping belts.

Conservation

When Singapore achieved independence in 1965, the economy was in shambles. Like many other developing nations, it put urban renewal and economic progress on the front burner; anything that stood in the way, from historic neighbourhoods to colonial architecture, was simply razed. As a result, by the 1970s it had achieved prosperity, but was criticised for its lack of character and culture.

In the 1980s the authorities began to restore buildings in four conservation areas: Boat Quay, Little India, Kampong Glam and Chinatown/Tanjong Pagar. Since then, more temples, buildings, shophouses and warehouses have been spared the wrecking ball. The gentrification, apart from giving the city added charm, has also helped Singaporeans develop a sense of their own history.

Public housing

In land-scarce Singapore, providing housing for the masses means building skywards. More than 80 percent of Singaporeans own and live in high-rise flats built by the Housing and Development Board. In many other parts of the world, public housing is associated with poverty and social unrest, but not in Singapore. Its public housing programme is in fact one of its finest achievements, with other fast-growing countries seeking to emulate its success.

Shoppers at Bugis Junction

Garden city

Singapore packs in quite a bit despite its minuscule size. Once you have covered the city centre, venture out to the suburbs, where the housing heartlands are interspersed with quirky theme attractions as well as forest reserves and other pockets of greenery.

The city's vast green zones surprise many first-time visitors, at least those expecting to find a sterile and air-conditioned metropolis of glass and steel. There is a legion of green belts, such as parks nestled between skyscrapers, offering respite in the concrete jungle. Four gazetted nature reserves – Central Catchment, Bukit Timah, Sungei Buloh and Labrador – together comprise over 3,340 hectares (8,250 acres) of untouched greenery, which is by no means slim pickings for this land-scarce city.

Getting around

Street signs are clear and the city is relatively easy to navigate. The various districts can be easily explored by bus, Mass Rapid Transit (MRT) trains or on foot, although the weather can get hot, humid and possibly uncomfortable for some. Taxis are comfortable, inexpensive and especially good for journeys to destinations in the suburbs.

MELTING POT

Singapore is home to about 5.4 million people, comprising 74.2 percent Chinese, 13.3 percent Malays, 9.2 percent Indians, with the remaining 3.3 percent made up of Eurasians, Arabs, Jews and other minority groups.

The lingua franca is English, but on the streets you will see Chinese, Malay, Indian, Eurasian and Caucasian faces. Singapore has been a migrant society since day one, and continues to receive new immigrants from the world over today. Mosques, churches, and Hindu and Chinese temples often stand side by side, and cuisines borrow ideas and ingredients from one another.

Four official languages are used in multicultural Singapore: English, Mandarin, Malay and Tamil. The language of administration is English. On the streets, you will hear different languages and dialects being spoken, including Singlish, a patois that combines English, Malay and Chinese dialects, which most Singaporeans identify with.

Preoccupations

The country tends to be overly competitive, thanks to a *kiasu* (meaning 'afraid to lose' in the Chinese Hokkien dialect) attitude. Singapore is always in a big hurry to chase grand dreams and strive for success, and has already made itself the world's busiest port and the second largest oil refiner, as well as home to what is often voted the globe's best airline and airport. The ambition to be No. 1 in everything it does is perhaps driven by a sense

Playing draughts in Chinatown

Having a Singapore Sling at the Raffles. This famous cocktail packs a delightful fruity punch. After a hot day in the sun, sip the iconic, chilled concoction at Raffles Hotel's Long Bar, where the drink was created in 1910. See page 35.

Discovering Peranakan culture. Learn more about the Peranakan or Straits Chinese culture at the Peranakan Museum, where lavish artefacts and exhibits are presented. Experience more of this unique culture over at East Coast Road, a veritable living museum dotted with Peranakan restaurants and cultural galleries. Don't forget to try some colourful, steamed Nonya cakes. See page 39.

Strolling around Gardens by the Bay. The sprawling gardens are home to two massive conservatories filled with lush greenery as well as a dozen Super Trees. The Singapore Garden Festival held here showcases creations by international acclaimed garden and floral designers. Look out for other seasonal floral exhibits such as Tulipmania and War of Roses. See page 45.

Cruising down the river in a bumboat. Hop on a bumboat which takes you down the Singapore River. Enjoy views of gleaming skyscrapers juxtaposed with colonial-era buildings, restored conservation warehouses, historical bridges, and riverside sculptures. See page 46.

Exploring ethnic neighbourhoods. The eclectic ethnic districts of Chinatown, Kampong Glam and Little India are microcosms of multicultural Singapore. Put on your walking shoes and soak up their colourful atmospheres on foot. Sample some authentic local cuisines in between your trails. See pages 68 and 72.

Tucking into chilli crab. In the food haven of Singapore, one would be hard pressed to name its national dish, but the spicy-sweet chili crab is one of the strongest contenders. Among the best places to savour this dish are the restaurants at the East Coast Centre. See page 119.

Prowling with nocturnal animals. A diverse range of animals roams freely in the subtly lit and naturalistic enclosures of the Night Safari. This is a rare chance to catch creatures that are active only at night. But before it turns dark, be sure to visit River Safari, where two of China's giant pandas have made their home. See page 97.

Soaking in the views at the Sands SkyPark. Head up to the highest level at Marina Bay Sands to take snapshots of the city. There is an observation deck, landscaped gardens and a one-of-a-kind infinity pool with amazing views of the skyline. See page 45.

Christmas at Orchard Road. Between November and December, this whole stretch is illuminated with sparkling lights and Christmas decorations. Splurge, window shop or simply experience the festive atmosphere at this mile-long shopping belt. See page 58.

East coast café life

of insecurity and the need to get the attention of and connect to the world beyond its limited shores, though the positive result of this is that the city has become a well-oiled, efficient machine.

Keeping up with the Joneses is also a major preoccupation of Singaporeans. At housewarming parties queries on the cost of the house and renovation are earnestly entertained. A compliment on a nice watch or a piece of jewellery will almost always be followed by a question on its price and provenance. If you are asked questions on money, don't be fazed; no rudeness or intrusiveness is intended.

Pastimes

When removed from their workaday world and indulging in their favourite pastimes, Singaporeans do let up and have fun. Without a doubt, the most well-loved activity is eating. The island's cultural diversity has given it a mind-boggling array of food options; as a result, this city never stops eating, even into the wee hours of the morning. Shopping ranks only a close second as Singaporeans' favourite diversion. Many indefatigable locals have been known to trawl Orchard Road on the weekends, mall by mall.

A CHANGING CITY

Singaporeans joke that if they leave the country for more than three months, they will not be able to recognise many places on their return, so relentless is the pace of change. Today the city is undergoing a renaissance of epic proportions. A new financial district and a revitalised waterfront has given it an extra boost and tourist arrivals have been increasing, thanks to the opening of two casino resorts – known as Integrated Resorts – and a Universal Studios theme park. There were concerns that the casinos in these resorts would encourage gambling, so Lee Hsien Loong suggested that safeguards should be implemented. As a result, Singaporeans and permanent residents pay an entrance fee of S$100 per visit or S$2,000 annually.

The city, once derided as boring compared to other Asian metropolises, is also learning to take itself less seriously. Its nightlife scene pulses with a wealth of genuinely cool bars and clubs, both imported and home-grown. And if the vibrant arts calendar is anything to go by, its appetite for high culture and entertainment is definitely growing.

But change is manifest not only in the physical landscape. If some of the people you meet seem less than gracious (despite the national kindness campaign), it is often because they are in a hurry, under the constant pressure to change for the better, 'upgrade' and improve themselves. For many, time is perhaps the greatest luxury in the rush for a better future.

In the heart of Chinatown

TOP TIPS FOR VISITING SINGAPORE

Child's play. The Jacob Ballas Children's Garden (Tue–Sun 8am–7pm; free), in the Botanic Garden's Bukit Timah Core, is a playground and nature park for kids. Adults can enter only if accompanied by a child below 13 years old or by a guide. At the zoo's Rainforest Kidzworld, children can hop on animal rides, run loose at a water playground and watch animal shows.

Festive seasons. October or November is one of the best times to visit Little India, as the whole place is dressed and lit for the Festival of Lights celebrations. In September and October every year, Chinatown and the Chinese Garden at Jurong are ablaze with pretty lanterns for the annual Mid-Autumn Festival celebrations.

Park Hopper. If you plan to visit the Singapore Zoo, River Safari, Night Safari and Jurong Bird Park, buy multi-park tickets such as the 4-in-1 Park Hopper ticket to get a lower combined price. The ticket is valid for one month from the date of purchase. You may visit each park on a different day. For Park Hopper options with Jurong Bird Park, Singapore Zoo or Night Safari, the ticket prices include tram rides.

Sentosa entrance fees. If you take the Sentosa Express to the island, the entrance fee is included in the fare of S$4. You can also enter the island via Sentosa Express using the ez-link card. If you walk via the Boardwalk, the entrance fee is S$1. Those who take a taxi will be charged either S$2, $3, $5 or $6 per taxi depending on the time and day. Most of the individual attractions have separate admission fees, which can add up if you are bringing your family, so take advantage of 'package' tickets with entrance to multiple attractions at discounts. Call 1800-736 8672 or visit www.sentosa.com.sg for more information.

Pricey booze. Expect to pay S$10 or more for a pint of beer and S$12–14 for house pours. Premium beers cost about S$15 to 20 a pop, and a bottle of bubbly around S$100. All bills are tagged with a 10 percent service charge and 7 percent tax. Take advantage of happy hour discounts or one-for-one deals, usually from 5–9pm.

Southern Islands overnight. Those who want to experience an overnight stay on St John's Island can book the Holiday Bungalow, which comes with a kitchen and houses 10 persons, or the Holiday Camp, which can accommodate up to 60 persons. Bookings and immediate payment must be made personally at the Sentosa Express station at VivoCity (tel: 1800-736 8672; daily 9am–8pm). For overnight camping (bring your own equipment) on Sisters' Islands and Pulau Hantu, you must obtain prior approval from Sentosa (email: administrator@sentosa.com.sg). There are no food and drink vendors on the islands, except Kusu during the pilgrimage season. It might be a good idea to pack a picnic when visiting these islands.

A food festival feast

FOOD AND DRINK

Singapore's cultural diversity has resulted in a vibrant food scene and a veritable explosion of flavours. With a mind-boggling array of options that cater to different tastes and budgets, you will never go hungry on this island.

Eating is a great passion in Singapore and life revolves around food. Singaporeans talk about food all the time and debate on where to get the freshest crabs, the spiciest chilli sauce or the best chicken rice – for hours on end and preferably over a meal. At the many food courts and hawker centres peppered all over the island, you can sample different cuisines in a single venue freshly cooked by an array of vendors.

Every imaginable cuisine is represented on this island, from refined Japanese and piquant Korean to robust Thai and exotic Middle Eastern. There are also excellent fine-dining restaurants, including Modern European, and traditional French and Italian.

CHINESE CUISINE

For just Chinese cuisine alone, a wide range of authentic restaurants can be found in Singapore – including those that serve the regional cuisines of China and food of different dialect groups.

Delicate dim sum, double-boiled soups and roasted meats are prepared in the Cantonese kitchen, while hearty meat dishes are rustled up by Hokkien cooks. Refined Teochew dishes usually comprise light, wholesome flavours such as steamed seafood and clear soups. The Hakkas are famous for their *yong tau fu* or beancurd stuffed with fish paste, and home-spun dishes flavoured with potent home-made rice wine.

The tongue-numbing Sichuan and robust Hunan food, both known for their liberal use of hot chilli peppers, as well as strongly flavoured Shanghainese and fine Beijing dishes are some of the many regional cuisines one can savour here.

INDIAN CUISINE

The Indian kitchen is largely divided into South and North Indian. South Indian meals mainly consist of fiery curries, aromatic *biryani* rice cooked with meat or seafood, as well as vegetarian *thosai* (rice pancakes) served with lentils. Several Indian restaurants in Singapore are well known for serving spicy southern fare on banana leaves.

North Indian cuisine is famous for its flavoursome tandoor grills, mild and rich curries, as well as fluffy *naan* breads. Meanwhile, the Keralan table features a host of seafood dishes.

Chicken satay is a favourite

Laksa, a typical local dish

Indian chefs often use a blend of spices such as cardamom, cloves, cumin and coriander to enliven their dishes. Yoghurt is sometimes added to North Indian curries to temper the spices, whereas coconut milk is used to mellow the intensely hot South Indian ones.

A hybrid Indian-Muslim food is usually found in hawker stalls around the island. Some familiar specialities are *roti prata* (a flaky griddle-fried bread eaten with curry), as well as *murtabak* (like *roti prata*, but stuffed with shredded chicken or mutton, sliced onions and egg).

MALAY CUISINE

Singaporean Malays are descendants of settlers from the Malayan Peninsula or Indonesia's Java and Sumatra islands. Mention Malay cuisine and one usually thinks of *nasi padang* (rice and assorted meat and vegetable side dishes) and spicy curries. These dishes usually include an assortment of spices and herbs such as ginger, turmeric, galangal, lemongrass, curry leaves, chillies and the ubiquitous *belacan* (a pungent shrimp paste). These dishes are often balanced with coconut milk, which takes the edge off the heat.

Nasi padang originates from Padang in West Sumatra. The many *nasi padang* eateries dotted around the island usually offer a wide variety of spicy meat and vegetable dishes served with white or turmeric-flavoured rice. At hawker centres, visit Malay stalls for the perennial favour-

ite, satay. Aromatic bamboo skewers of marinated beef, mutton or chicken are grilled over hot charcoal and served with sliced onion, cucumber, rice cakes and a piquant spicy and sweet peanut sauce.

PERANAKAN CUISINE

A unique cuisine that deserves special mention is Peranakan, or Nyonya, cooking. Peranakans are descendants of early immigrants from China who settled in 19th-century Penang, Melaka and Singapore and married local Malay women. Peranakan cuisine originates from the fusion of Malay and Chinese culinary styles.

To impart a distinctive flavour and aroma to their rich curries and stews, chefs add the essential *rempah* mixture – fragrant herbs and spices such as lemongrass, chillies, shallots, candlenuts, *belacan* (shrimp paste) and turmeric ground by hand in a pestle and mortar. Tamarind paste, coconut milk and *taucheo* (fermented beans) are also used to liven up the robust concoctions. Dishes often require long hours of slow

Food and drink prices

Price guide for a meal for one (excluding drinks and taxes):

$$$$ = over S$60
$$$ = S$40–60
$$ = S$20–40
$ = below S$20

Tempting crispy prawns

cooking and complicated preparations; flavours are complex and can range from fiery to delicate.

Desserts – in the form of little cakes called *nyonya kueh* – are colourful, sweet and sticky: perfumed with coconut cream and pandan leaves, and sweetened with dark and syrupy palm sugar.

Although best eaten in a Peranakan home, this cooking can be enjoyed in a handful of restaurants in Singapore. Look out for dishes such as *ayam buah keluak*, which combines chicken with earthy Indonesian black nuts to produce a rich, thick gravy as well as beef *rendang*, a spicy, dry beef stew that is often simmered for hours until fork tender.

SINGAPORE'S SIGNATURE DISHES

Over the years, several unique delicacies have evolved to tantalise the local tastebud. These dishes are particularly close to the hearts of Singaporeans.

Hainanese chicken rice
This iconic dish was first introduced by immigrants from China. Succulent and juicy chicken meat poached in stock is served with fragrant rice that has been steamed with ginger, garlic and chicken stock. The chicken and rice are served with dips – vinegary chilli sauce, ginger paste and sweet black soy sauce.

Fish-head curry
This speciality is unique to the Indian community. Massive fish heads are stewed in a gravy alongside eggplant, tomatoes and okra. The meat is succulent and the gravy, spicy and intense. Aficionados say the cheeks, lips and eyes are the best parts of the fish head.

Chilli crab
Singaporeans will tell you that this dish is best made with giant Sri Lankan crabs. The thick, tangy and spicy gravy is mopped up with fried or steamed *mantou* (Chinese buns).

Laksa
Thick rice noodles bathed in a rich and spicy coconut gravy jazzed up with herbs, and crowned with sliced fish cake, tofu, cockles, prawns and beansprouts.

BREAKFAST

A typical Singaporean breakfast usually means heading to a coffee shop for a dose of freshly grilled *kaya* toast – bread spread with butter and a sweet coconut jam made from sugar, eggs and coconut cream, and flavoured with pandan leaves. To complement the stacks of crispy *kaya* toast, one can also order soft-boiled eggs drizzled with soy sauce and a cup of thick black coffee.

DRINKS AND DESSERTS

An iconic drink is *teh tarik* or 'pulled tea'. Tea sweetened with condensed milk is poured from cup to pitcher and back again to ensure that the concoction is

Lau Pa Sat Festival Market

well mixed and frothy. A variation is the soothing *teh halia* or ginger tea, a staple at Indian drink vendors. In hawker centres and at food courts, try freshly squeezed fruit juice, cold soya bean milk or sugar cane juice.

Delicious food needs something worthy to wash it down with, and the locally brewed Tiger and Anchor beers are excellent choices. Don't leave without tasting a Singapore Sling – a zesty blend of gin, cherry brandy, Cointreau, pineapple juice and fresh lime.

To end your meal, try *cendol* or ice *kacang* – shaved iced desserts with red beans and jelly, topped with syrup and coconut milk or evaporated milk.

HAWKER CENTRES

Hawker centres are scattered all over the island. Always a hive of activity, the scores of Malay, Chinese and Indian stalls offer a wide variety of traditional fare at low prices that will not bust your budget. Some of the most popular hawker centres are Lau Pa Sat Festival Market, Maxwell Road Food Centre and Newton Food Centre. From dawn until dusk, row upon row of stalls bustle with hawkers dishing out their specialities. Regulars often throng these places in search of their favourite stalls. Every evening, Boon Tat Street beside the Lau Pa Sat Festival Market becomes a pedestrian-only street and is transformed into an atmospheric haunt for satay lovers. Hawkers grill skewered meat over burning charcoal and serve them with rice cakes and a tangy peanut sauce dip.

The local hawker centres are always packed during lunch and dinner, so head there earlier if you don't have the patience or time to wait for a table. However, communal sharing of tables is common during busy hours – simply smile and ask the person at the table if you can share it. If you are with a group at a hawker centre, have one person sit at a table to reserve the seats. The others, having noted the table number, should order their food and tell the hawkers where they are seated.

Cookery classes

There are a handful of established cookery schools in Singapore. at-sunrice (28 Tai Seng Street, Lift Lobby 2, Level 5; www.at-sunrice.com) offers demonstrations, tasting classes and hands-on cooking classes in Asian cuisine. Cookbook author Shermay Lee, at Shermay's Cooking School (Chip Bee Gardens, Blk 43 Jalan Merah Saga, #01-76; www.shermay.com), imparts Peranakan secrets based on her grandmother's traditional recipes. Palate Sensations (Chromos #01-03, 10 Biopolis Road (opposite Buona Vista MRT and MOE Building); www.palatesensations.com) is an open concept studio offering a range of hands-on cooking classes. Asian, Italian, Chinese and French cuisines are taught by the resident executive chef and other guest chefs.

Luxury brands at ION Orchard

SHOPPING

Singapore's shopping scene is red-hot. New malls sprout at breakneck speed while older ones receive makeovers. The choice ranges from Orchard Road's shiny, glitzy shopping centres to charming shophouses in the ethnic enclaves.

Shops in Singapore are generally open daily from 10–11am to about 9pm, so you can literally shop till you drop. Some malls in Orchard Road open till late on Friday and Saturday nights. Although there are no distinct sales periods that follow the seasons, stores generally mark down their prices periodically. The best time to shop is from late May to early July during the annual Great Singapore Sale. Post Christmas and Chinese New Year are also good for bargains.

Note that there is a 7 percent Goods and Services Tax (GST) on most purchases in Singapore, for which tourists can claim refund for purchases above S$100 at the airport before departure.

SHOPPING DISTRICTS

Orchard Road

Orchard Road is to Singapore what Fifth Avenue is to New York. Even people who have never been to Singapore have heard of Orchard Road – such is its claim to shopping fame. The area is a shopaholic's dream – one dazzling mall after another filled with swanky department stores and any number of retail outlets and designer boutiques. There are malls dedicated to young children (Forum The Shopping Mall), adolescents (Far East Plaza), antique and carpet fiends (Tanglin Shopping Centre) and the moneyed (Hilton Gallery, ION Orchard, Ngee Ann City and The Paragon), along with the usual shopping centres selling all manner of goods.

Marina Bay

The mega-sized Suntec City Mall has countless shops selling clothes, shoes, bags, electronic equipment, books and sports apparel. Adjoining it is a subterranean shopping mall called CityLink Mall, which conveniently connects to the City Hall MRT station, Marina Square and the Esplanade Mall, part of the Esplanade – Theatres on the Bay.

The Shoppes at Marina Bay Sands boasts over 800,000 square feet of retail and restaurant space. You can indulge in a unique luxury shopping experience here; brands include Hermès, Chanel, Prada and Gucci.

Civic District

Funan DigitaLife Mall is the place to find computer equipment and software. Above the City Hall MRT station is Raffles City, a

Souvenir shopping in Chinatown

six-storey mall with a wide array of retail outlets. Just opposite on North Bridge Road is Raffles Hotel Shopping Arcade, with a clutch of designer boutiques.

Kampong Glam

Arab Street is where to go for fabrics and handwoven baskets. The shops here are piled high with leather bags, baskets and rattan goods, purses and shoes. Haji Lane, lined with vintage boutiques and local designers' shops, is one of Singapore's hippest shopping streets.

Little India

Serangoon Road and the neighbouring side streets are a treasure trove of spices, jewellery, Indian silk and more from the subcontinent. Mustafa Centre at Syed Alwi Road is a large 24-hour shopping mall crammed with low-priced electronic goods and other bargains. Little India Arcade comprises colourful restored shophouses stuffed with interesting paraphernalia.

Chinatown

For all things Chinese, visit the tiny shops along Pagoda Street and Temple Street, and the stalls at the Chinatown Night Market. Nearby Yue Hwa Emporium sells exquisite Chinese silk and handicrafts like teapots and fans.

WHAT TO BUY

For purchasing photographic equipment, prices are attractive but it's best to get an international guarantee. If you want to take a risk on imported goods intended only for the local market, you can save on the price. Being such a wired country, Singapore is also a good place to purchase both hardware and software. The law comes down hard on bootleg software and frequent raids are carried out at shopping malls specialising in computers – so buy the genuine stuff and ask for a guarantee.

Watches are sold tax-free, and the choice is endless. Gold jewellery is also a good buy. Traditional designs crafted in 22K yellow gold are available at jewellers in Serangoon Road and Chinatown, while more contemporary pieces in 18K white or yellow gold set with precious or semi-precious stones are sold at local chains like Gold Heart and Lee Hwa in the shopping centres. International jewellers like Tiffany and Cartier have boutiques in Singapore too. More unique are orchid blooms – sold under the Risis brand – plated with 22K gold to preserve their beauty and crafted into jewellery.

Home-grown fashion designer Ashley Isham has his own plush store at Mandarin Gallery and Orchard Central. Other local names of note are project-shopbloodbros, M)Phosis and Bodynits.

The range of antiques and handicrafts from Bangkok, Borneo and beyond is vast. There are baskets from the Philippines, Buddha images from Myanmar, Indian brassware, Chinese ceramics and more. Ask for a certificate of authenticity if you buy the genuine stuff.

Live music

ENTERTAINMENT

Once described as bland and banal, the island's nightlife scene has gone up a few hip notches in recent years. Whether you want to catch a live show, have a no-holds-barred night of bar-crawling or go clubbing, the choices are plentiful.

Party-goers in Singapore are a capricious lot, so the scene reciprocates with overwhelming variety and venues that open (and close) at a furious rate, though established hotspots continue to pack in the crowds year after year.

WHERE TO GO

Nightspots are scattered all over the island, but there are a few key areas where you can spend an entire night hopping from one venue to another:

Singapore River: The nightlife hubs along the river are a quick taxi ride from one another. The bars and pubs set in conservation shophouses on Boat Quay are popular with tourists and executives from nearby Raffles Place. Upriver from Boat Quay, Clarke Quay sizzles with party-goers in the flashy bars and clubs set in restored 19th-century warehouses.

Orchard Road: The main shopping strip of Orchard Road is home to classy hotel lounges and bars with live performances. At its southern end is Emerald Hill, which has charming pubs patronised by expats and creative types.

Chinatown: A few streets in Chinatown area buzz with hip independent bars. These include Keong Saik Road, Jiak Chuan Road, and the ever popular Club Street and Ann Siang Hill.

Sentosa and Surroundings: The beachside bars dotted on the island resort of Sentosa, such as Tanjong Beach Club, are fantastic places for knocking back cocktails. Opposite Sentosa and adjacent to VivoCity shopping mall is St James Power Station, a massive entertainment complex housed in a former coal-fired power station.

Further Afield: A number of relaxing drinking holes are also worth exploring in more secluded enclaves. One prime example is Dempsey Hill, located near Singapore Botanic Gardens, where you will find some stylish al fresco bars and restaurants housed in former British army barracks and set amid lush greenery.

HOTEL BARS

If you don't fancy a noisy street of bars and clubs, hotel bars are good alternatives. Swissôtel the Stamford has the vertigo-inducing New Asia Bar on its 71st floor, while Raffles Hotel's Long Bar is the progenitor of the gin-based Singa-

Dancing the night away at the Pump Room

pore Sling. Another good option is the smart Post Bar at the Fullerton Hotel; its menu includes a dizzying array of martinis. The Grand Hyatt's plush Martini Bar is also a top draw for its range of alcoholic concoctions.

CLUBS

Zouk, on Jiak Kim Street, is the island's most well-known dance club. It is part of the international clubbing circuit and plays edgy underground and house music. There are talks about Zouk's closure when the lease ends, but for now it's still one of the top hotspots in town. Attica/Attica Too, at Clarke Quay, are home-grown favourites where DJs spin everything from hip-hop to electronic beats. Butter Factory at One Fullerton is another fashionable clubbing hotspot. Most dance clubs have strict dress codes: no slippers, shorts or singlets, and certainly no drugs.

Gay venues
The pink crowd gather in Tanjong Pagar, where there is a clutch of gay clubs and bars. Popular choices include dance clubs Taboo, and laidback bars like Tantric and Does Your Mother Know (or popularly known as DYMK).

LIVE ENTERTAINMENT

For such a tiny city, Singapore has a fantastic range of live entertainment.

Rock and pop music
The best places to listen to Singapore musicians and bands are The Pump Room at Clarke Quay, Timbré at The Substation and Wala Wala Café Bar in Holland Village. They perform pop and rock covers as well as original works.

Jazz
For an evening of jazz, head to Boat Quay's Harry's Bar or Arab Street's Blu Jazz Café. These have diverse line-ups of local bands as well as international jazz acts.

Classical music
The Singapore Symphony Orchestra performs mainly mainstream classics at their weekly concerts at the Esplanade Concert Hall. Look out, too, for performances at the refurbished Victoria Theatre & Concert Hall.

Theatre and dance
Singapore's lively English-language theatre scene features a mix of Broadway favourites and musicals like *Wicked* as well as local productions of original works. Companies include Wild Rice, TheatreWorks, The Necessary Stage and Singapore Repertory Theatre.

The dance scene is headlined by the Singapore Dance Theatre, whose repertoire ranges from the classics to contemporary ballet set to pop music. Another company to look out for is Arts Fission, whose edgy productions draw inspiration from Asian heritage.

The Chingay parade marks the end of Chinese New Year festivities

FESTIVALS AND EVENTS

Multicultural Singapore is a constant hive of activity, celebrating one festival after another. Almost every month of the year, Singapore's streets, temples and ethnic enclaves come alive with an assortment of religious and cultural celebrations.

JANUARY TO MARCH

Chinese New Year: The most widely celebrated festival among the Chinese, it falls on the first day of the lunar calendar, usually between mid-January and mid-February. The 15-day festival, beginning with a two-day holiday, is commemorated by feasting and the giving of hong bao, red packets of 'lucky money'. Catch the festive spirit in Chinatown.

Thaipusam: This Hindu festival is observed between January and February. Devotees honour Lord Muruga by performing feats of mind over spirit. The festival begins at dawn at the Srinivasa Perumal Temple in Serangoon Road. Here, devotees who have entered a trance have their bodies pierced with metal hooks or spikes attached to a *kavadi*, a cage-like steel contraption which is carried on their shoulders. The procession makes its way to the Sri Thandayuthapani Temple at Tank Road.

APRIL TO JUNE

Vesak Day: Usually celebrated in May, this is the most important event in the Buddhist calendar, for it honours the birth, death and enlightenment of Buddha. Temple celebrations begin at dawn with a candlelight procession. As part of the celebrations, caged birds are released and free meals are distributed to the poor.

Dragon Boat Festival: The festival honours a Chinese patriot, Qu Yuan, who drowned himself in 278 BC to protest against the corruption of the imperial court. Small packages of rice were thrown into the water to distract fishes from his body, and villagers decorated their boats with dragon heads and tails with the same purpose in mind. Today, several varieties of these rice dumplings are sold at Chinese restaurants and top hotels.

JULY TO SEPTEMBER

Singapore Food Festival: This month-long food fiesta in July holds various food-tasting events and unique dining experiences.

National Day: The National Day Parade on 9 August, features pomp and pageantry to celebrate the city-state's independence, and culminates in a stunning fireworks display. Held at the Padang traditionally, National Day will be celebrated

Deepavali rituals   *Singapore National Day flypast*

at the new Sports Hub at Kallang in 2016. 2015 marks Singapore's 50th year of independence, celebrated with a whole spectrum of events, including exhibitions and special walking trails.

Singapore Night Festival: For two weekends in August, the art and heritage district of Bras Basah comes alive at night with stunning outdoor light installations, as well as music, dance, art and aerial performances.

Singapore International Festival of Arts: This annual six-week event in August and September showcases Asian and Western performing arts from dance and theatre to music.

Formula 1 Singapore Grand Prix: This night race is held at the Marina Bay area over a weekend in mid-September. There are also plenty of entertainment and concerts held during the Grand Prix season.

OCTOBER TO DECEMBER

Mid-Autumn Festival: This traditional harvest festival takes place on the 15th day of the eighth lunar month, usually in October. Mooncakes – pastries filled with lotus paste or red bean paste – are presented as edible gifts. Don't miss the impressive display of colourful lanterns in Chinatown.

Sri Mariamman Temple on South Bridge Road. Male devotees sprint barefoot across glowing coals in honour of Draupathi, a legendary heroine deified by South Indian Tamils.

Deepavali: Also known as the Festival of Lights, to symbolise the conquest of good over evil, this is the most important festival in the Hindu calendar. Usually occurring in October or November, Little India is a hive of activity and turned into a fairyland of twinkling lights.

Christmas: Almost everyone, regardless of religious affliation, gets into the spirit of exchanging gifts come Christmas time. Orchard Road is transformed into a riot of lights and glitzy displays, while shopping malls and hotels try to outdo each other with the most imaginative decorations.

Hari Raya Puasa: This Muslim celebration falls on the first day of the 10th Muslim month; the date varies from year to year. During Ramadan, the month preceding Hari Raya Puasa, all able Muslims observe a strict fast from sunrise to sunset. On Hari Raya Puasa, celebrants ask for forgiveness from family members, and feast on traditional food. Apart from the festival light-up at Geylang Serai, another hub of activity during the Muslim Hari Raya Puasa is Kampong Glam.

2015 SEA Games

The 28th Southeast Asian Games (SEA Games; www.seagames2015.com) is a biennial multi-sport event involving participants from the current 11 countries of Southeast Asia. 2015 marks the fourth time that Singapore have hosted the games (the last was in 1993), with 36 sports and 402 events staged at the new Kallang Sports Hub.

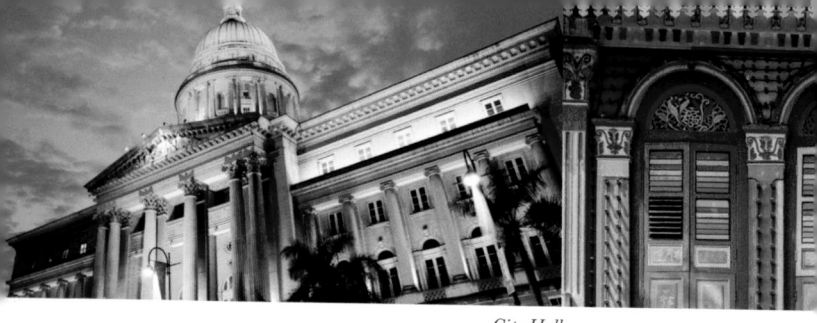

City Hall

HERITAGE ARCHITECTURE

There are some gems to discover among Singapore's architecture, from the Civic District's grand and elegant colonial buildings and meticulously restored traditional shophouses, to iconic modern landmarks.

Singapore's architecture showcases a spectrum of influences and styles from different periods. Over the past two decades, conservation efforts have been carried out to preserve Singapore's architectural heritage. This includes the restoration of historic buildings and adapting them for new uses. Examples are The Fullerton Hotel (formerly the General Post Office) and the National Art Gallery, which takes over the old Supreme Court building in 2015. Meanwhile, the Peranakan-style mouldings and ornate decorations of shophouses are kept intact in places like the Koon Seng Road stretch (Joo Chiat Road) and Emerald Hill.

SHOPHOUSES

Of all the architectural styles in Singapore, none is as distinctive as the lavishly decorated shophouses found in the city's older neighbourhoods. Known as Chinese Baroque or Singapore Eclectic architecture, these shophouses sport a rich mix of Malay, Chinese and European architectural details. The shophouse was so called because the lower floor was used for business while the upper level served as living quarters.

The design, initiated by Raffles, had detailed specifications to achieve conformity. They were arranged in a linear form and built of masonry with tile roofs. Linking the shophouses was a covered path called the 'five-foot way' because the width between the building and the street had to be exactly five feet. Over the years, five distinct shophouse styles developed, many of which have been restored to their original splendour.

The Early style was the first shophouses, erected in the 1840s, with their squat upper levels and simple lines. Dating to the early 1900s, the First Transitional shophouses added an extra floor to maximise space. The Late style dating from 1910 to the late 1930s is the most florid of all styles, with lavishly decorated facades. The Second Transitional style from the late 1930s onwards combined Asian and European architectural influences, including Malay-style wooden eaves, Corinthian columns and pilasters and French windows with timber louvres. Art Deco is the most recent of styles, mainly built between 1940 and 1960. It is the most European in character; a private forecourt area with a gate and a balcony on the upper floor are typical features.

Colourful shophouses   *Marina Bay Sands*

Many old shophouses are much sought-after these days because of their unique facades and historical value. Strict guidelines govern the restoration of shophouses, many of which have been turned into restaurants, bars and offices.

COLONIAL BUILDINGS

Another significant collection of historic buildings are those built by the British during the colonial period. These structures generally feature Neo-classical, Palladian and Renaissance styles. Some of the most prominent examples include the Fullerton Building, the old Parliament House, the old Supreme Court Buildling, City Hall, the Victoria Theatre and Concert Hall, National Museum of Singapore, Hill Street Central Fire station, Raffles Hotel and Chijmes. Some of the city's main churches also feature the gothic style, including St Andrew's Cathedral and the Cathedral of the Good Shepherd, both in the City Hall district.

Aside from these grand structures, there are also charming 19th century black and white bungalows in lush neighbourhoods such as Rochester, Tanglin Road, and Portsdown. Homes of top ranking government officials and the army during the colonial days, these were abandoned after the British left. Today, there are about 500 of these buildings left. Most have been renovated into beautiful residences and rented to expats, or leased to artists, architects and designers.

MODERN ICONS

Singapore's skyline has changed dramatically over the past decade and today brims with gleaming skyscrapers and one-of-a-kind masterpieces. Iconic landmarks have sprouted around town since the government introduced the two integrated resorts in 2010. Moshe Safdie's Marina Bay Sands, featuring three lofty towers crowned by a massive SkyPark and massive infinity pool, is the most talked about engineering wonder in the city. Other unique structures in the area include the white lotus-shaped Art Science museum and Gardens by the Bay's Flower Dome and Cloud Forest. Before these were built, Esplanade – Theatres on the Bay with its colossal dome-shaped structures was the highlight. It remains a significant landmark today.

Preserving Tiong Bahru

Unique pre-war architecture can be seen at the old housing estate of Tiong Bahru, about five minutes taxi ride from Outram and Chinatown. A 'Streamline Modern' architecture style with sweeping, aerodynamic lines is incorporated into some of these buildings and the designs are reminiscent of trains, ocean liners and aeroplanes. The post-war flats here are inspired by the International style. Today, Tiong Bahru's buildings are highly sought-after. A number of independent cafes have also set up shop here.

HISTORY: KEY DATES

From a tiny fishing village to a pivotal trading post at the crossroads of the East and West, to the Asian economic powerhouse it is today, Singapore's evolution owes much to its inhabitants' ingenuity and hard work.

BRITISH COLONIAL RULE

1819	Sir Stamford Raffles sets up a trading post for the British East India Company with the agreement of the Sultan of Johor and the Temenggong, his representative on the island.
1824	The Sultan cedes Singapore in perpetuity to the British.
1826	Singapore, with Malacca and Penang, becomes part of the Straits Settlements, under the control of British India.
1867	The Colonial Office in London takes over control of Singapore.
1911	The population of Singapore grows to 250,000 and the census records 48 races on the island, speaking 54 languages. It becomes the greatest naval base of the British empire east of Suez.
1942	The Japanese invade and occupy Singapore.
1945	The Japanese surrender and the Allied Forces return.

POST-WORLD WAR II

1946	Singapore becomes a Crown Colony.
1948	The British allow limited elections to the Legislative Council. A state of emergency is declared in June, following the Malayan Communist Party's uprising against British imperialism.
1955	The Rendel Constitution granted by the British leads to general elections.
1956	People's Action Party (PAP) Central Executive Committee elections, in which the Communists decline to run, are held. Chinese students riot; PAP leaders are arrested.
1958	Singapore is granted partial independence.
1959	At the first general elections for a Legislative Assembly, PAP's Lee Kuan Yew becomes prime minister.
1963	Singapore joins the Federation of Malaysia.

British troops surrender to the Japanese in 1942

| 1964 | PAP wins only one seat in the Malaysian general elections. Racial riots take place. |

INDEPENDENCE

1965	Singapore withdraws from the Federation and becomes a republic. It joins the United Nations and the Commonwealth.
1967	Singapore, Malaysia, Thailand, Indonesia and the Philippines form the Association of Southeast Asian Nations (ASEAN).
1968	In the first general elections, PAP wins all 58 seats.
1987	The US$5 billion Mass Rapid Transit (MRT) system opens.
1990	Lee Kuan Yew steps down after 31 years as prime minister and hands the reins over to Goh Chok Tong. The constitution is amended to provide for an elected president.
1991	PAP wins the elections, but loses four seats to the opposition.
1993	Ong Teng Cheong is Singapore's first elected president.
1999	S.R. Nathan from the minority Indian community is appointed president.

21ST CENTURY

2002	The landmark Esplanade – Theatres on the Bay opens. Al Qaeda-linked terrorist plot to bomb the US embassy uncovered. Some 15 suspects are arrested and jailed without trial.
2003	Outbreak of Severe Acute Respiratory Syndrome (SARS) in April.
2004	Lee Hsien Loong becomes Singapore's third prime minister.
2008	The Singapore Flyer, the world's tallest observation wheel, opens. The world's first Formula 1 night race is held.
2010	Singapore's Integrated Resorts open.
2011	The general elections are held in May and the ruling People's Action Party (PAP) wins with their lowest ever ratings of 60 percent since independence. Soon after, Lee Kuan Yew announces his retirement from cabinet. S.R. Nathan steps down as president and Tony Tan is elected.
2012	The sprawling Gardens by the Bay with its Super Trees and conservatories are unveiled.
2015	Singapore hosts the 2015 SEA games and ASEAN paralympic games.

BEST ROUTES

City Hall

CIVIC DISTRICT

Many of the historical buildings in the Civic District have been restored and adapted for contemporary functions, but the genteel colonial elegance of the area remains unmistakable.

DISTANCE: 2.5km (1.5 miles)
TIME: Half a day
START: St Andrew's Cathedral
END: Raffles Hotel
POINTS TO NOTE: Take the MRT to the City Hall station and turn left after the fare gates.This brings you to the side entrance of St Andrew's Cathedral. If you take a taxi, ask the driver to stop at the taxi stand at Raffles City Shopping Centre and then cross the road to the church.

In his town plan of 1822, Stamford Raffles designated the area north of the Singapore River as the colonial hub, ordering the building of offices, banks, hotels, churches and clubs. The area, roughly between the City Hall and Dhoby Ghaut MRT stations, is now known as the Civic District.

ST ANDREW'S CATHEDRAL

Grab a bite at **Tiong Bahru Bakery**, see ❶, in Raffles City. This I.M. Pei-designed complex comprises a shopping mall, the 72-storey Swissôtel the Stamford and the 26-storey Fairmont Singapore. Beneath the complex is the City Hall MRT station, which is linked via the subterranean CityLink Mall to Suntec City and the Esplanade – Theatres on the Bay.

After having your coffee fix, start your journey at the graceful **St Andrew's Cathedral** ❶ (www.livingstreams.org. sg; Mon–Sat 9am–5pm, and Sundays 7am–9pm). This English Gothic-style church was built by Indian convict labourers, who used a special plaster known as Madras *chunam*, made of egg white, egg shells, lime, sugar and coconut husk, to achieve the gleaming white exterior. The structure you see now is actually the second church to be built on this site, designed by Ronald MacPherson and consecrated in 1862. The earlier Palladian-style building was struck by lightning twice and demolished in 1852.

Architecturally significant and steeped in history, the cathedral has, befittingly, been gazetted as a national monument. Note the pretty stained-glass windows

St Andrew's Cathedral

behind the altar. Known as the East Windows, the three panels are dedicated to Stamford Raffles, John Crawfurd, the second resident of Singapore, and Major General William Butterworth, a governor of the Straits Settlement. Behind the pulpit is the Coventry Cross, formed by nails salvaged from the ruins of England's Coventry Cathedral, which was destroyed during World War II.

THE PADANG

A diagonal path leads from the cathedral to the green expanse known as the **Padang** ❷ ('field' in Malay), along St Andrew's Road. Known as the Esplanade in colonial times, this was where the Europeans played cricket and socialised in the cool of the evenings. In 1942, during the Japanese Occupation, European civilians were rounded up on the Padang and forced to march 22km (14 miles) to Changi, where they were imprisoned. Today the Padang plays host to public events and rugby and cricket matches.

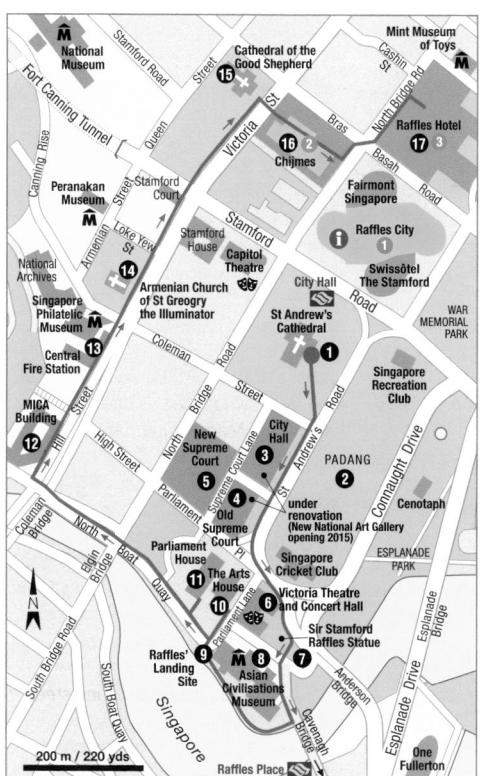

On either side of the Padang are private clubs, the venerable Victorian-style **Singapore Cricket Club** to your right and the newer **Singapore Recreation Club** to your left.

CITY HALL

Across St Andrew's Road from the Padang are two handsome structures that used to be Singapore's

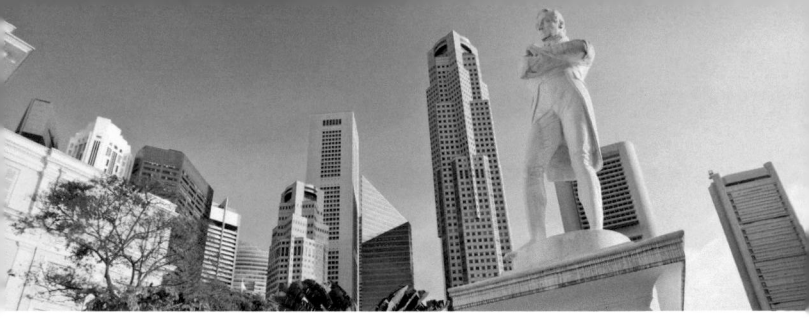

most important government buildings. In 1945 Lord Louis Mountbatten accepted the Japanese surrender on the grand staircase of the **City Hall ❸**, which was completed in 1929. It was also here, in front of the grand Grecian columns, that Lee Kuan Yew declared Singapore's self-government status in 1959 and the country's independence in 1963.

Court buildings

Next to the City Hall is the green-domed **Old Supreme Court ❹**, built in 1939. Of note is the tympanum sculpture by Italian sculptor Cavalieri Rudolfo Nolli. He is said to have used his daughter as his model for the centre figure of Justice, which is flanked by figures representing a lost soul, the law, gratitude, prosperity and abundance.

The Old Supreme Court and City Hall buildings are currently being converted into the **National Art Gallery** (www.nationalartgallery.sg), opening in 2015. To mark the opening, there will be a 10-day long festival which will include programmes at the Padang. Looming right behind is the glass-and-steel **New Supreme Court ❺**, capped by a futuristic disc. The observation deck on the 8th floor (free) has good views of the city.

VICTORIA THEATRE AND CONCERT HALL

Cross Parliament Place and past the Old Parliament House to the **Victoria Theatre** and **Victoria Concert Hall ❻** (www.

vtvch.com), which are linked by a landmark clock tower. Although the two neoclassical buildings were designed to match, the theatre – completed in 1862 as a town hall – predates the 1902 concert hall. After undergoing major renovations, the theatre and concert hall re-opened in July 2014. Since 1979, Victoria Concert Hall – an important performing space for theatre, dance and music – has been home to the Singapore Symphony Orchestra.

For the centenary of Singapore's founding in 1919, a bronze **statue of Sir Stamford Raffles ❼**, cast by T. Woolner, was relocated from the Padang to the Victoria Memorial Hall, now the Victoria Concert Hall. It was moved to the National Museum during World War II and thereafter returned to the forecourt of the concert hall in 1946.

ASIAN CIVILISATIONS MUSEUM

From the theatre and concert hall, move on to the **Asian Civilisations Museum ❽** (www.acm.org.sg; Sat–Thu 10am–7pm, Fri 10am–9pm) on Empress Place. The original building was completed in 1865 and designed in Neoclassical style by J.F. McNair. Be sure to devote enough time to this wonderful museum, which has 11 galleries. Its diverse collection of artefacts, from prehistoric agricultural tools to textiles and bronzeware, reveal Asia's cultural and historical complexities.

In the China Gallery, displays such as Chinese deities and fragile Dehua porce-

The Chamber at The Arts House.

lain are the highlights, while the Koran-inspired calligraphic art in the West Asia Gallery is impressive. The South Asia galleries hold religious statuary and architectural motifs of the Indian subcontinent.

RAFFLES' LANDING SITE

Continue on the leafy promenade by the Singapore River to the **Raffles' Landing Site ❾**. Here stands another statue of Stamford Raffles, a white marble replica of the original in front of the Victoria Concert Hall, which marks the spot on the northern bank where the man first stepped ashore on 28 January 1819. There are fine views of Boat Quay and the Central Business District across the river.

THE ARTS HOUSE

Adjacent to the Raffles' Landing Site is **The Arts House ❿** (www.theartshouse. com.sg; daily 10am–10pm; free), a multi-disciplinary arts centre occupying the former Parliament House, which was built in 1827. The building was originally designed to be the private residence of a wealthy merchant. It was instead used as the first Court House and Assembly House, and then by the Parliament until 1999. In its grounds is a bronze elephant statue, a gift from King Chulalongkorn of Siam in 1871. The Arts House has a busy schedule of film screenings, art exhibitions, and theatre and dance performances. Its 200-seat performance space, named the Chamber, was where mem-

bers of parliament debated bills and laws in the past. Today they parley at the austere **Parliament House ⓫** just behind.

MICA BUILDING

If you decide to call it a day, cross Cavenagh Bridge to the Raffles Place MRT station. If you are keen to explore the Civic District further, then walk by the riverside to Elgin Bridge; on its right is an underpass that takes you to North Boat Quay. Cross the road to Hill Street, on which stands the **MICA Building ⓬**, the Renaissance-style headquarters of the Ministry of Information, Communications and the Arts. The building, erected in 1934 with 911 technicoloured window shutters, used to be the Old Hill Street Police Station. On its ground floor is the **ARTrium**, with several art galleries showcasing the works of local and Asian artists.

Turn left as you exit the MICA Building and walk along Hill Street. Next to the building is a steep staircase, which leads up to **Fort Canning Park** (see page 36).

CENTRAL FIRE STATION

Further along is the **Central Fire Station ⓭**, the oldest fire station in Singapore, housed in a fine example of the 'blood and bandage' architectural style, completed in 1901. This style, with alternating exposed brickwork and whitewashed plaster, is a departure from the usual Palladian and classical styles prevailing in Singapore at the time.

Civil Defence Heritage Gallery

The fire station also houses the **Civil Defence Heritage Gallery** (www.scdf.gov.sg; Tue–Sun 10am–5pm; free), a unique museum with displays of antique fire engines and interactive stations depicting firefighting operations. On the guided tour, you get to climb up the hose tower, the lookout point in the early days.

ARMENIAN CHURCH

Across Coleman Street from the fire station is the **Armenian Church of St Gregory the Illuminator** (http://armeniansinasia.org; daily 9am–6pm), the oldest church in Singapore, built in 1835. This is where Singapore's small Armenian community congregates on Sunday. The tombstones of prominent Armenians in Singapore's history lie in its memorial garden. Among them are the tombstones of the Sarkies brothers who founded the Raffles Hotel, and Agnes Joaquim, who discovered the orchid hybrid *Vanda Miss Joaquim*, now Singapore's national flower.

CATHEDRAL OF THE GOOD SHEPHERD

At the intersection of Victoria Street and Bras Basah Road on the left is the **Cathedral of the Good Shepherd** , the oldest Roman Catholic church in Singapore and a national monument. Completed in 1846, it was designed by Denis Lesley Sweeney. Its architecture recalls that of England's St Martin-in-the-Fields and St Paul's in Covent Garden, while the three bells in the steeple were cast by the Auguste Hildebrand Foundry in Paris. In its grounds is the residence of the current Archbishop of Singapore, a simple two-storey bungalow with a portico and enclosed verandahs.

CHIJMES

Opposite the cathedral across Victoria Street is the restaurant and entertainment hub **Chijmes** (www.chijmes.com.sg), pronounced 'chimes'. The Gothic-style buildings were formerly occupied by the Convent of the Holy Infant Jesus (CHIJ), founded in 1854. The Sisters on the Seine from France ran a school with boarding facilities for girls and an orphanage, which took in babies left at its Gate of Hope on Victoria Street.

The conversion of a convent school and religious building into a nightlife

Mint Museum of Toys

Across from the Raffles Hotel, on Seah Street, is the Mint Museum of Toys (tel: 6339 0660; www.emint.com; daily 9.30am–6.30pm; charge), a trove of rare toys, from vintage Popeye the Sailor and Felix the Cat to superheroes like Batman and Superman, put together by Chang Ya Fa. To date he has accumulated some 50,000 pieces, estimated to be worth S$5 million, from auctions and curio shops around the world.

Mint Museum of Toys   *Cloister at Chijmes*

hub was not without controversy, but it is generally agreed that the restoration was tastefully done; the mouldings in the chapel and along the walkway are especially beautiful, and the fountain courtyard is a pleasant place for a break. Peek into the old chapel, which has exquisite stained glass. A good place for lunch here is **Lei Garden**, see ❷.

RAFFLES HOTEL

Exit Chijmes at the intersection of Bras Basah and North Bridge roads. Diagonally opposite Chijmes is the last stop of your tour, the legendary **Raffles Hotel** ⓱ (http://singapore.raffles.com). Built in 1887 by the Sarkies brothers and restored in the 1990s, the hotel has welcomed numerous famous personalities over the years. Somerset Maugham summed up its spirit best when he said the 'Raffles stands for all the fables of the exotic East'. The genteel air of this national monument is still palpable today and is best soaked up in the leafy courtyard with antique fountains. The **shopping arcade** has bespoke tailors, antiques stores, and luxury boutiques of brands like Tiffany & Co., Coach and Louis Vuitton.

The Raffles Hotel has good options for the night. There may be performances at its **Jubilee Hall**. After dinner at one of its many restaurants, have a quiet drink at the **Bar & Billiard Room**, which carries a nice selection of cigars, and still has the very billiard table under which, so the story goes, the last tiger in Singapore was

shot. For something less formal, there is the raucous **Long Bar**, the only place in Singapore where you can toss peanut shells onto the floor with impunity. This is where you can try the famous Singapore Sling, first created as a lady's cocktail in 1910 by bartender Ngiam Tong Boon.

But for now, after your tour of the Raffles, have tea at **Ah Teng's Bakery**, see ❸.

Food and drink

❶ TIONG BAHRU BAKERY
B1-11/12 Raffles City Shopping Centre; tel: 6333 4160; daily 8am–10pm; $$
This popular outlet, a partnership between Gontran Cherrier, Parisian celebrity baker, and Singapore's Spa Esprit Group, serves French-style baked goods with a twist. It's a good spot for coffee and croissant.

❷ LEI GARDEN
01-24 Chijmes; tel: 6339 3822; daily 11.30am–3pm, 6–11pm; $$$
This venerable Chinese restaurant serves well-executed dim sum for lunch alongside fresh seafood, barbecue pork, roast duck and other Cantonese specialties.

❸ AH TENG'S BAKERY
Raffles Hotel; tel 6412 1816; daily 7.30am–6pm; $$
This cosy old-school café is excellent for afternoon tea. On the menu are local snacks, salads, sandwiches and cakes.

Waxwork exhibit at The Battle Box

MUSEUM DISTRICT

Tiny Singapore has a disproportionally large number of museums, located all over the island. Thankfully for the visitor, the major ones, such as the National Museum, Peranakan Museum and Singapore Art Museum, are conveniently clustered in the Civic District in a zone known as the Museum District.

DISTANCE: Varies, depending on the number of museums visited
TIME: A full day
START: Raffles City
END: Singapore Art Museum
POINTS TO NOTE: Take the MRT to the City Hall station and head to the Raffles City Shopping Centre for breakfast.

Among Singapore's many museums, there are historical ones that catalogue the island's early stories through artefacts and war relics; art and design museums that showcase cutting-edge creativity; and quirky repositories that display unique tastes. This route brings you to four museums, each offering different insights into the city's heritage.

A good breakfast option in the area is **Cedele Depot**, see ❶, in Raffles City. After breakfast, exit the mall and walk down Stamford Road, past **Stamford House** which is currently being re-developed into a luxury hotel.

Turn left onto Hill Street, pass the Armenian Church and turn right onto Canning Rise, which brings you to **Fort Canning Park**.

FORT CANNING PARK

Explore **Fort Canning Park** ❶ on its well-marked paths. History abounds on Fort Canning Hill, once known as Bukit Larangan (Forbidden Hill) as commoners were not allowed here. Archaeological excavations indicate that the Malay princes who ruled Singapore in the 14th century had sited their palaces here. Stamford Raffles also built his residence here in 1823, as the hill offered good vantage for keeping watch on Singapore's coast. In 1860 the British built a fort, from which cannon fire announced dawn, noon and dusk daily.

The hill also holds an old tomb said to contain the remains of Iskandar Shah, the last ruler of pre-colonial Singapore. This has been consecrated as a Muslim *keramat* (shrine).

Behind the whitewashed Fort Canning Centre is **The Battle Box** (currently undergoing maintenance until further notice). The bunker, with a maze-like

Peranakan Museum

complex of rooms and corridors 9m (30ft) underground, was constructed in 1936 as the nerve centre of British military operations in Southeast Asia. The Battle Box is a museum chronicling the fall of Singapore to the Japanese during World War II through exhibitions created with audio and visual effects, animatronics and lifelike waxwork. It was here on 15 February 1942 that British officers made the decision to surrender. Adjacent to The Battle Box is a 1926 building that served as an army barracks; it now houses Hotel Fort Canning and The Legends Fort Canning Park country club.

Walk down the patch of green known as Fort Canning Green, which used to be an old Christian cemetery until 1865, towards the entrance that is marked by two Gothic gates. Leave the park and walk down Canning Rise towards Coleman Street, past the Registry of Marriages. On your left is **The Singapore Philatelic Museum ❷** (23B Coleman Street; www.spm.org.sg; Mon 1–7pm, Tue–Sun 9.30am–7pm), which offers a unique window onto Singapore's history. It has displays of postcards, first-day covers and stamps from the private collections of renowned philatelists.

Silk bridal gown at the Peranakan Musuem

PERANAKAN MUSEUM

After popping into the stamp museum, turn into Armenian Street where the **Peranakan Museum ❸** (www.peranakan museum.org.sg; daily 10am–7pm, Fri until 9pm) is located. The building that houses the Peranakan Museum was formerly occupied by the Tao Nan School. Set up by Hokkien immigrants to preserve their cultural heritage, it was the first school in Singapore to use Mandarin as the medium of instruction.

This museum was the first in the world dedicated to Peranakan heritage and material culture. Peranakans, or Straits Chinese, have a fascinating hybrid culture that has evolved since the 17th century and years of intermarriage between immigrant Chinese men and local Malay women in the former British Straits Settlements of Singapore, Malacca and Penang.

Peranakan life and heritage are thematically presented in 10 permanent galleries. Themes include the origins of the Peranakans, the fastidious 12-day Peranakan wedding, the role of the Nonya, the Peranakan woman, as well as Peranakan cuisine, which is a major preoccupation in the culture.

Two notable exhibits are located in the **Wedding Gallery**. A 19th-century silk bridal gown, adorned with embroidered phoenixes and peonies, is typical of that worn by Peranakan brides in Singapore and Malacca. Another major exhibit is the wedding bed, ornately carved with auspicious motifs and decorated with embroidered hangings and beads. The wedding bed is traditionally one of the largest pieces of furniture in the homes of wealthy Peranakans.

The **Food and Feasting Gallery** presents glimpses into the unique Peranakan cuisine and dining customs. Elaborately set up here is a *tok panjang* (long table), laden with colourful porcelain of all shapes and sizes, used for the traditional 12-course feast held during weddings and special occasions.

THE SUBSTATION

Leave the museum and walk down Armenian Street. At no. 45 is **The Substation ❹** (www.substation.org), an independent arts centre converted from a disused power station. Its small theatre is often the stage for experimental drama and dance productions. Peep into the gallery; there may be an ongoing exhibition of an emerging visual artist. In the garden of The Substation, you will find Timbre Music Bistro (www.timbre.com.sg; daily 6pm–1am, Fri–Sat until 2am), a popular live-music venue with great pub grub and local musicians performing nightly.

NATIONAL MUSEUM

At the end of Armenian Street, cross the road to Stamford Road and turn left after the Singapore Management University's School of Accountancy on your left. Further ahead on the left is the **National**

Historical photographs at the National Museum

Museum ❺ (www.nationalmuseum.sg; Singapore History Gallery daily 10am–6pm, Singapore Living Galleries daily 10am–8pm; charge; free daily 6–8pm). Before you tour the museum, have lunch at **Flutes**, see ❷.

Opened in 1887, the original building was designed by J.F. McNair as the former Raffles Library and Museum. Designed in elegant neo-Palladian style, the building was expanded in 1906, 1914 and 1916. The museum emerged from another major facelift, the most extensive reconstruction and conservation project in its history, in late 2006.

The building, now restored to its former splendour, has a new glass-and-steel wing, whose star attraction is the beautiful **Glass Rotunda**. Designed as a modern interpretation of the original **Rotunda Dome**, the glass rotunda lights up like a lantern at night, with projected images that depict Singapore's history.

For the original Rotunda Dome's restoration, experts took down its curved stained-glass panels, which were then restored by a professional stained-glass artist who used 18th-century reinforcement techniques. The Victorian floral and square patterns remain as vivid as ever after the stained-glass pieces were buffed and cleaned. Go up on the four-storey **Glass Passage** to view the dome's exterior architectural details such as elegant Palladian motifs and 19th-century fish-scale zinc tiles.

The museum will undergo a $10 million facelift from the last quarter of 2015.

Galleries

There are two main sections in the National Museum: the **History Gallery** and four **Living Galleries**. The history section traces Singapore's past from the 14th century to the present day through two complementary 'paths' that chronicle key events and everyday experiences of citizens.

The Living Galleries afford insights into everyday life in modern Singapore through its engaging fashion, film, food and photography sections. In the **Food Gallery**, for example, you can find out more about Singapore's street food from the 1950s to 1970s: Not only do you see and 'hear' the installations, you

Peranakans

Peranakan men are known as *baba* and the women *nonya*. They were the first locals to speak English and adopt Western customs during the colonial times. In fact their loyalty to the British led some to describe them as the 'King's Chinese'. They speak a Chinese-Malay patois, and their culture is derived from the traditions of these ethnic groups. Most perceptibly Peranakan culinary heritage is a blend of Malay and Chinese cooking styles and ingredients. Many Peranakan families used to reside in Emerald Hill and Katong in terrace houses that sport a distinctive architectural style. Having intermarried with other races, Peranakans are becoming less distinct as a racial group.

Displays in Singapore National Museum

can also catch whiffs of the different types of food and spices.

The **Exhibition Galleries** are where temporary exhibits are staged. A prominent past exhibition featured 130 classical Greek and Hellenistic artefacts from the Louvre in Paris.

National Treasures

Don't forget to look out for the 10 'National Treasures'. These historically significant and rare artefacts, selected from the National Museum's collection, date from the 14th century to the mid-20th century.

One important relic of the country's pre-colonial history is the **Singapore Stone**, located in the Singapore History Gallery. It is engraved with the earliest inscription found on the island. What you can see in the museum is the remains of a large boulder that originally stood by the Singapore River, near where the Fullerton Hotel stands now.

The boulder split into three parts after it was blown up in the 19th century for the widening of the river. The full inscription, dating from the 10th to the 14th century, has not been deciphered as scholars cannot agree on the date of origin and the language, which has however been speculated to be a variant of an old Sumatran script.

Another highlight in the History Gallery is the 19th-century **will of Munshi Abdullah**, who is known as the Father of modern Malay literature. A contemporary of Stamford Raffles and Colonel William Farquhar, he is most well known for his magnum opus *Hikayat Abdullah (The Story of Abdullah)*, which contains his firsthand impressions of the island after 1819, the year Sultan Hussein of Johor allowed the British East India Company to establish a trading post in Singapore. Munshi's will, dating to 1854, is a rare document, as wills were uncommon during his time.

The museum has an excellent Chinese puppetry collection, of which the **Xin Sai Le Puppet Stage**, found in the Film and Wayang Gallery, is another interesting National Treasure. Chinese puppet shows were a popular form of street entertainment for immigrants from the 19th to the early 20th century. This glove-puppet theatre stage, with 1,000 light bulbs, belonged to the Xin Sai Le troupe from the Fujian province in South China, which visited Singapore in the 1930s. The whole theatre could be dismantled or assembled within an hour by the troupe. The collection comes with 45 puppets, 96 costumes, 56 hats, 24 pieces of backdrops, accessories and 20 pieces of props, stored in two wooden chests.

SINGAPORE ART MUSEUM

From the National Museum, cross Stamford Road to Bencoolen Street, walk past the buildings of the Singapore Management University and turn right. Further along on Bras Basah Road is the **Singapore Art Museum** ❻ (www.singaporeartmuseum.sg; daily 10am–7pm, Fri until 9pm).

Contemporary art in the Singapore Art Museum

Historical building

Hailed as a national monument, the 1855 museum building once housed the St Joseph's Institution, a Catholic boys' school founded in 1852 and run by the La Salle Brothers. After 135 years on Bras Basah Road, the school was relocated in 1987 and the building was sensitively restored as Singapore's national art museum. Note the former chapel, now the museum's auditorium, featuring a stained-glass installation by Filipino contemporary artist Ramon Orlina. Original architectural features that have been retained include the pretty courtyards, shuttered windows and ceramic floor tiles.

Collection

Institutional and private collectors in Singapore avidly amass art from the region, and this museum is one of them. It has an excellent sampling of works by leading Asian artists, such as Affandi and Hendra Gunawan from Indonesia and Chinese Nobel Prize laureate Gao Xingjian.

The museum also holds the Singapore's national art collection. The permanent collection of over 7,500 artworks includes representative works of well-known local artists such as Liu Kang and Georgette Chen. One highlight is Chen's *Still Life with Orange and Apples*. The museum has acquired 94 of her paintings, which comprise portraits, still lifes and landscapes.

The museum's café, **Dome**, see ❸, is good for afternoon tea.

Food and drink

❶ CEDELE DEPOT

03-28A Raffles City Shopping Centre; tel: 6337 8017; Mon–Fri 11am–10pm, Sat 9am–10pm, Sun 9am–9pm; $$
This outlet of a home-grown bakery chain serves a great all-day breakfast. Fill up with the hearty Big Breakfast Set with brioche or white toast, bacon, sausages, scrambled eggs and mushrooms. No less decadent are the wild blueberry pancakes with vanilla butter and maple syrup, and the chocolate French toast

❷ FLUTES

The National Museum of Singapore, 93 Stamford Road; tel: 6338 8770; www.flutes.com.sg; Mon–Fri 11.30am–2pm, Mon–Sat 6.30-10pm, Sunday roast 11am–2.30pm, weekend brunch 10am–2.30pm, afternoon tea Fri–Sun 3–5pm; $$$$
This restaurant relocated from the former Hill Street Fire Chief's residence to the National Museum. Dine on modern European flavours and pair the dishes with wines from the extensive drinks list.

❸ DOME CAFÉ

01-01 Singapore Art Museum; tel: 6339 0792; www.olio.sg; Sun-Thur 8.30am–10.30pm, Fri-Sat until 11pm; $$
Seats outside offer views of the museum's quaint courtyard with fountains. On the menu are cakes, pastries, tarts and gelati.

MARINA BAY

Singapore's newer iconic structures such as the Marina Bay Sands, the Esplanade Theatres, the Singapore Flyer and the Marina Bay Financial Centre dominate the ever-changing Marina Bay district.

DISTANCE: 3km (2 miles)
TIME: Full day
START: Esplanade
END: Helix Bridge
POINTS TO NOTE: Take the MRT to the City Hall station and turn right into CityLink Mall after the fare gates. Follow the signs to Esplanade. From there, you can explore the entire Marina Bay loop.

The Singapore River empties into the Marina Bay, an artificial inlet formed by reclaimed land. Marina Bay is also the name of the area around the bay, the city's new downtown. A landscaped promenade forms a continuous pedestrian route along the waterfront, linking the Esplanade to Collyer Quay and the Marina Bay Sands Integrated Resort.

THE ESPLANADE

Start your tour at **The Esplanade – Theatres on the Bay ❶**. The S$600 million Esplanade (www.esplanade.com), designed by British architect Michael Wilford and Singapore's DP Architects, was somewhat controversial when it was completed in 2002, with the spiny exterior of its two colossal dome-shaped auditoriums often compared to the thorny husks of the durian fruit. Singaporeans have, however, grown to love the bold architecture.

If time permits during your visit, make sure to catch a performance here. The 1,600-seat concert hall and 2,000-seat theatre have outstanding acoustics. The well-regarded **Singapore Symphony Orchestra** performs its season at the concert hall; tickets are available at the box office (daily noon–8.30pm).

After your Esplanade tour, have early lunch at **No Signboard Seafood**, see ❶, at the Esplanade Mall. If you return here for an evening performance, try hawker fare at the **Makansutra Gluttons Bay** outside the mall.

ESPLANADE PARK

From the mall, exit onto the **Marina Bay Promenade**. Walk along the waterfront; the view of the CBD skyline from here

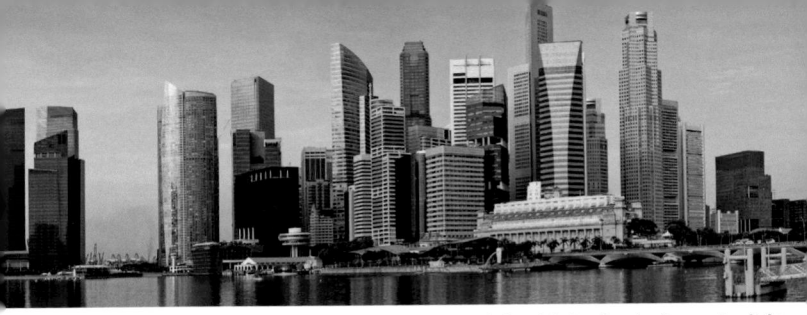

is fantastic. Continue under the **Esplanade Bridge** to the **Esplanade Park ②**, a green belt along Connaught Drive.

At the park's northern end is the Victorian-style **Tan Kim Seng Fountain**, constructed to mark the merchant's contribution in 1857 to build the town's water works. The **Cenotaph**, whose granite surface is engraved with the words 'Our Glorious Dead', is dedicated to the 124 British men who lost their lives in World War I. After World War II, more inscriptions were added on the other side of the

Merlion Park

stone. At the southern end is the **Lim Bo Seng Memorial**, dedicated to the war hero who led the anti-Japanese resistance movement, Force 136, during World War II.

Head onto the pedestrian path along Anderson Bridge. Ahead is the Art Deco-style **Fullerton Waterboat House** ③ (1919), so named because it supplied water to ships anchored out at sea. Restored with its original curved facade intact, the building now houses a rooftop bar and Boathouse Restaurant.

MERLION PARK

Just before the Waterboat House, turn left and follow the path to the **Merlion Park** ④. By the water's edge is a 8.6m (28-ft) -high statue of the water-spewing Merlion. First unveiled in 1964, the tourism icon has a lion's head, which recalls the myth of ancient Singapore's founder Sang Nila Utama, said to have spotted a lion on the island around the 14th century. Its fish tail symbolises the city's beginnings as a fishing village.

FULLERTON BUILDINGS

Next to the Merlion Park is the glass-and-steel **One Fullerton** ⑤, with a clutch of restaurants and cafés offering alfresco, waterfront seating.

The **Fullerton Hotel** ⑥ is linked by an underpass to One Fullerton. It occupies a 1924 building named after Robert Fullerton, the first governor of the Straits Settlements, and a fine example of the Edwardian Baroque neoclassical style that once dominated the Civic District. Before it was restored and reopened as a hotel in 2001, the building was the heart of social and commercial life as the Chamber of Commerce and the General Post Office.

COLLYER QUAY

The Fullerton Waterboat House, Fullerton Hotel and One Fullerton make up a leisure precinct known as **Fullerton Heritage**, which also comprises the **Collyer Quay** area, further south along the waterfront. The re-developed **Customs House** ⑦ today houses The Fullerton Bay Hotel, several restaurants and bars with stunning views of the bay. From Customs House, walk along the waterfront promenade which links to **Marina Bay Sands**.

Singapore Flyer

On the same side of the bayfront as the Esplanade is the 165m (540-ft) -high Singapore Flyer (www.singaporeflyer.com; daily 8.30am–10.30pm). When it opened in 2008 it displaced the London Eye as the world's highest observation wheel. Unobstructed in all directions, the giant wheel offers panoramic views of Malaysian and Indonesian islands as well as Singapore's city skyline, which is particularly scintillating at night.

Fullerton Hotel

Supertree Grove at Gardens by the Bay

MARINA BAY SANDS

The centrepiece of this area is the massive **Marina Bay Sands ⑧** (www.marina baysands.com) – the most expensive development ever built by the American casino-resort giant, Las Vegas Sands. This 'integrated resort' has transformed Singapore's skyline since it was completed in 2010; the mega leisure, entertainment and hospitality complex features a casino, luxury hotel, convention facilities, high-end boutiques, a theatre, nightclubs, bars and restaurants.

One of the many 'engineering wonders' here is the 200-m **Sands Sky Park ⑨**, a fascinating structure designed by architect Moshe Safdie. Perched on top of the three lofty hotel towers are a sweeping 1.2-hectare tropical park with landscaped gardens, an observation deck, and an infinity pool with amazing views of the skyline.

To the west of Marina Bay Sands Integrated Resort is the **Marina Bay Financial Centre**, an extension of the CBD.

GARDENS BY THE BAY

Across the highway via a pedestrian bridge is an area called **Gardens by the Bay ⑩** (www.gardensbythebay.org.sg; daily 5am–2am outdoor gardens, 9am–9pm conservatories and OCBC Skyway) featuring two lush conservatories: Flower Dome, with a controlled 22°C environment, and Cloud Forest, which boasts the world's tallest indoor waterfall. There is

also a dozen towering Supertrees offering shade in the day and glittering light display at night. Two of the Supertrees are connected by the OCBC Skyway, affording views of the sprawling area.

Adjacent to Marina Bay Sands complex is the **Art Science Museum ⑪** (open daily 10am-10pm; charge). The unique white coloured lotus-shaped building houses galleries exhibiting art, science, media, technology, design and architecture.

Another engineering masterpiece nearby is the world's first **double helix curved bridge ⑫** which allows pedestrians to walk across from Marina Bay Sands to the other side of the waterfront. This bridge affords beautiful sunsets and views of the bay from its look-out points. You can end your tour at the **Youth Olympic Park ⑬**, an 'art park' with creative installations by local youth. It is right at the end of the Helix Bridge and near the Floating Stadium. Alternatively, walk to the foot of the Singapore Flyer and have a meal at the 1960s-themed food street.

Food and drink

① NO SIGNBOARD SEAFOOD
01-14/16 Esplanade Mall; tel: 6336 9959; www.nosignboardseafood.com; daily 11am-11pm; $$
This well-established restaurant serves white pepper crab, Hokkien style steamed fish, crispy cereal prawns and a range of fresh seafood creations

SINGAPORE RIVER

The Singapore River is where the city's modern history began. Take a trip along the river down memory lane, to see colonial-era bridges, stately buildings and conservation shophouses that reflect the city's past.

DISTANCE: 1.5km (1 mile)
TIME: 3–4 hours
START: Merlion Park
END: Clarke Quay or Merlion Park
POINTS TO NOTE: Walk from the Raffles Place MRT station to the Merlion Park or take a taxi to One Fullerton, which is next to the park. This is recommended as an afternoon-to-evening tour. You can combine this tour with route 3 (see page 42).

Spanning almost 4km (2.5 miles) from its mouth at Marina Bay to Kim Seng Bridge on the other end, the Singapore River was the island's commercial lifeline for more than a century, where Stamford Raffles and early immigrants first landed. The swamps and floating skulls deposited by pirates are now long gone, as are the coolies, junks and warehouses and its quays are lined by colourful conservation shophouses and warehouses.

River cruise
A leisurely way to enjoy the sights along the banks is to board the **Singapore**

The curve of Boat Quay represents the belly of the carp, an auspicious shape

River Experience (www.rivercruise.com.sg), a pleasant 30-minute cruise on an environmentally-friendly electric bumboat, designed to look like a traditional one of yesteryear. Purchase your ticket (daily 9am–10.30 pm) at the Singapore River Cruises & Leisure booth at the jetty at the **Merlion Park ❶**. The boat wends its way from Marina Bay (see page 42) to Boat Quay and Clarke Quay, passing under several bridges, and then turns around at the Liang Court jetty for the return journey to the Merlion Park. If you have more time, you can also opt for the 45-minute cruise, further upriver to Robertson Quay.

However, if you prefer to alight at any point along the river, such as at Clarke Quay as recommended in this route, purchase a one-way river taxi ticket The operator of the Singapore River Experience cruise runs a river taxi service that takes you from one point to another along the Singapore River. Rates depend on destinations. Let the attendants know in advance where you want to disembark. Buy your ticket and you will be able to board at any of the nine jetties along the Singapore River.

HISTORICAL BRIDGES

When you board the boat, be sure to take advantage of the good photo opportunities of buildings like The Esplanade – Theatres on the Bay (see page 42) and Fullerton Hotel (see page 42).

The Singapore River flows under 12 bridges, many of which are historical structures with beautiful designs. The cruise takes you under the first bridge, **Anderson Bridge ❷**, built in 1910 to link the colonial district (now the Civic District) and the commercial district (present-day Raffles Place).

You then pass under **Cavenagh Bridge ❸**. Made in Scotland and reassembled in Singapore, the bridge was named after Major-General Orfeur Cavenagh, Governor of the Straits Settlement from 1859 to 1867. It was originally planned as a drawbridge but upon completion was found to be appropriate only as a fixed structure. Now it serves a pedestrian bridge linking the north and south banks.

BOAT QUAY

As the cruise continues, to your left is **Boat Quay ❹**, which runs along the south bank between Cavenagh Bridge and Elgin Bridge. Boat Quay was a trading hub from the colonial days until the 1970s, when lighters were banned from the river, and flotsam and jetsam was cleared. Its shophouses, which held cargo in the early days, were restored to their former glory and updated as restaurants and bars.

Today's Boat Quay has seen better days, having been eclipsed by the revitalised Clarke Quay (see below). Neverthe-

Nightlife at Clarke Quay

less, its eclectic mix of alfresco eateries, lively Irish pubs and trendy bars still appeals to executives from the vicinity and tourists seeking to dine or drink by the river.

MORE BRIDGES

At the end of Boat Quay is **Elgin Bridge** ❺, named after the governor-general of India from 1862 to 1863, Lord James Bruce Elgin. The current concrete structure was completed in 1929 and replaced an earlier iron one brought in from India in 1862. The bridge was constructed as a link between the Chinese on the south side of the river and the Indian merchants of High Street on the north.

The cruise then passes under the concrete **Coleman Bridge** ❻. Its appearance today is a far cry from the original Palladian-style brick bridge designed by Irish architect George Coleman and built in 1840. The present concrete bridge opened in 1986 to better cope with heavy traffic flow.

The next bridge is **Read Bridge** ❼, built in 1889 and named after businessman and legislator William Henry Read. In the early days Chinese storytellers entertained Chinese coolies with classic tales of history and chivalry on this bridge.

RIVERSIDE POINT

If you have bought a river taxi ticket, alight at the Riverside Point jetty. **Clarke Quay Central** ❽ (www.clarkequaycentral.com.

sg; daily 11am–10pm) is a short walk away, and is a Japanese-themed mall with boutiques selling streetwear and accessories. Sip a cup of local tea at **Ya Kun Kaya Toast**, see ❶, or have a bite and drink at the restaurants at **Riverside Point** ❾, such as **Café Iguana**, see ❷, or **Brewerkz**, see ❸. Afterwards, cross Read Bridge to Clarke Quay.

CLARKE QUAY

Clarke Quay ❿, spanning five blocks, was named after Lieutenant-General Sir Andrew Clarke, the second governor of the Straits Settlement. Until the 1970s, it hummed with activity as bumboats carried cargo from ships to the warehouses on its banks.

Wander at will and look a little closer to discover some of its history. At its southern end, for instance, on the wall of the last shophouse is a sign proclaiming that it was once Whampoa's Ice House. A wealthy Chinese landowner, Whampoa gifted the land where the Singapore Botanic Gardens sits today to the British, who gave him the land at Clarke Quay in return.

Today's Clarke Quay hums to a different beat, with its restored warehouses housing restaurants and notable clubs like Attica (see page 121). The area is pleasant to stroll around in; huge canopies provide cool shade over its lanes in the day and are stunningly lit at night, while lily-pad platforms offer pleasant alfresco dining over the river. If you have

Robertson Quay

not had dinner, consider **The Pump Room**, see ④.

ROBERTSON QUAY

If you have opted for the 45-minute river cruise, your boat will head on to **Robertson Quay** ⑪. In the old days, this part of the riverbank was filled with warehouses. Now it has been mostly taken over by luxury apartments. The 19th-century warehouses that remain have been restored and are occupied by bars and restaurants.

The boat goes past the **Singapore Tyler Print Institute** ⑫ (www.spi.com.sg; Tue–Fri 10am–7pm, Sat 9am–6pm; free), a gallery with interesting print exhibitions.

Alkaff Bridge

After the print institute, the boat passes under the pedestrian **Alkaff Bridge** ⑬, named after the wealthy Arab Alkaff family. Completed in 1997, the bridge has been painted by the late Filipino artist Pacita Abad with help from a team of rope specialists, using 50 different colours and 900 litres of paint.

The boat turns around near the Grand Copthorne Waterfront hotel and then makes its way back to the Merlion Park.

Food and drink

① YA KUN KAYA TOAST
Clarke Quay Central #01-31; tel: 6534 7332; daily 7.30am–10pm; $
Have a cup of local tea or coffee at this outlet. If you are feeling peckish, order a crispy stack of kaya toast (toast with coconut jam).

② CAFÉ IGUANA
01-03 Riverside Point; tel: 6236 1275; www.cafeiguana.com; Mon–Thu 4pm–1am, Fri until 3am, Sat noon–3am, Sun noon–1am; $$
This lively restaurant is always packed, thanks to its delicious quesadillas, tortillas and salsas, and cheap margaritas during Happy Hour. It also offers over 150 types of Webber blue agave tequila.

③ BREWERKZ
01-05/06 Riverside Point; tel: 6438 7438; www.brewerkz.com; Sun–Thu noon–midnight, Fri–Sat until 1am; $$$
This microbrewery-restaurant produces over 2,500 hectolitres of handcrafted beer annually. American-style dishes from the Deep South, the Southwest and California are served.

④ THE PUMP ROOM
01-09/10 The Foundry, Clarke Quay; tel: 6334 2628; www.pumproomasia.com; Sun–Fri 5pm–3am, Sat 5pm–4am; $$$
The hearty Australian-inspired fare at this microbrewery and bistro include crispy blue swimmer crab cake, burgers and a variety of Australian steaks. Try the freshly brewed speciality beers.

CBD buildings

CENTRAL BUSINESS DISTRICT

The modern and the traditional collide and coalesce in Singapore's financial district. On this route, gaze at gleaming skyscrapers, admire quirky sculptures, view feng shui-friendly architectural features, and visit age-old places of worship.

DISTANCE: 2.5km (1.5 miles)
TIME: Half a day
START: Raffles Place
END: red dot design museum
POINTS TO NOTE: Start your tour after 9.30pm or 2pm to avoid the crowds.

The Central Business District runs close to the Marina Bay waterfront from the Singapore River to Keppel Road. Soaring towers of finance and business line its main arterials of Shenton Way, Robinson Road, Anson Road, Cecil Street and Battery Road. The tallest buildings are centred around **Raffles Place ❶**, a buzzing open-air plaza with the Raffles Place MRT station underground.

In the early days Raffles Place was known as Commercial Square, originally conceived by Stamford Raffles as part of his 1822 town plan. Grand structures housing banks and offices stood here, overlooking a landscaped centre with trees and flower beds. Also an important shopping destination for upper-crust society, Commercial Square was where

Singapore's first department store, Robinsons, was founded in 1858. Destroyed in a fire in 1972, it now has branches in Orchard Road (see page 62) and Raffles City (see page 30).

SKYSCRAPERS

A few notable skyscrapers surround Raffles Place, all measuring 280m (920ft) tall (the maximum height allowed by the aviation authorities): OUB Centre, Republic Plaza and UOB Plaza.

Japanese architect Kisho Kurokawa designed the dark, glazed **Republic Plaza ❷**, at the end of D'Almedia Street. This tapering tower won him the World Best Architecture Award from FIABCI in 1997.

From Raffles Place turn left onto Chulia Street. The twin towers of **UOB Plaza ❸**, one of the most recognised icons of the city skyline, were designed by another Japanese architect, Kenzo Tange. He fused his vision with that of Lim Chong Keat, his counterpart for the original octagonal 38-storey UOB Building, adding more levels that are turned

Incense coils at the Wak Hai Cheng Temple

at 45 degrees relative to one another, to give the building a unique chiselled look.

Continue on Chulia Street to South Canal Road. You will reach **OCBC Centre** ❹, designed by I.M. Pei. This 52-storey, the first foreigner-designed skyscraper after independence, was completed in 1976. Nicknamed 'the Calculator', it has three distinctive tiers separating windows that resemble but-

ton pads. Henry Moore's *Reclining Figure* (see page 52) stands in front of OCBC Centre.

Opposite OCBC Centre is Boat Quay (see page see page 47). On Circular Road stands **Molly Malone's**, see ❶, good for pub grub.

WAK HAI CHENG TEMPLE

After lunch, backtrack on South Canal Road and continue on Philip Street. At the corner with Church Street is the **Wak Hai Cheng Temple** ❺ (daily 6am-6pm), built in the 1850s by the Teochew community for the protection of traders travelling between Singapore and China. A constellation of deities, including Ma Chu Po, the Goddess of the Sea, and the Eight Immortals, are enshrined here. Suspended in the forecourt are large coils of incense, which can take up to 10 days to burn.

Cross Church Street to **Capital Square** ❻, an office block with a feature of cascading water, presumably installed to invite prosperity, for in Chinese belief, water is wealth.

200 m / 220 yds

Diorama at the Fu Tak Chi Museum

FAR EAST SQUARE

Take the path between Capital Square and China Street. Ahead is **Ya Kun**, see ❷, an institution for *kaya* (coconut jam) toast. Enter **Far East Square** ❼ by the Metal Gate, one of the complex's five gates, each representing an element of the Chinese universe: metal, wood, water, fire and earth.

Far East Square is a conservation area of restored shophouses in four archi-tectural styles prevalent from 1840s to 1960s – Early, First Transitional, Late and Second Transitional. Bounded by Cross, Telok Ayer and China streets, the complex houses mainly offices and restaurants.

Follow the signs, through a glass door, to the **Fu Tak Chi Museum** ❽ (daily 10am–10pm; free), formerly a Taoist temple set up by Hakka and Cantonese immigrants in 1824. It displays artefacts donated by early Chinatown residents.

Public art

A handful of sculptures are peppered around the CBD. Close to the riverside entrance of Raffles Place is Taiwanese sculptor Yang Ying-Feng's monumental *Progress and Advancement*, a celebration of the city's commercial life commissioned by the late banker Lien Ying Chow. Salvador Dali's bronze *Homage to Newton* is found in the ground-floor atrium of UOB Plaza. Just outside the atrium stands the voluptuous bronze Bird, by Columbian artist Fernando Botero, which was inspired by the dove, the universal symbol of peace. Ouside OCBC Centre is British sculptor Henry Moore's *Reclining Figure*. When it was first installed, it suffered from corrosion caused by the humid climate, and was subsequently treated to acquire the golden hue it wears today. There are also other bronze sculptures, which depict life in the early days, along the Singapore River.

TELOK AYER STREET

From the museum, turn right on Telok Ayer Street. Meaning 'water bay' in Malay, this street once stood by the shore. Its shophouses are mainly of the First Transitional style, with narrow fronts and modest ornamentation.

Nagore Durgha Building
At the corner with Boon Tat Street is the **Nagore Durgha Building** ❾, built in the late 1820s by Tamil Muslims as a meeting place and house of worship. With its intricate minarets, arches and niches, it has been described as a multilayered wedding cake.

Thian Hock Keng Temple
The next place of worship is the **Thian Hock Keng Temple** ❿, the Temple of Heavenly Happiness (www.thianhockkeng.com.sg; daily 7.30am–5.30pm). Hokkien immigrants set up a joss house in the 1820s in gratitude to Ma Chu Po for their safe arrival. This became the Thian

red dot design museum

Hock Keng, built in 1842 without a single nail. Dragons, venerated for protection on sea voyages, adorn the roofs and pillars.

Al Abrar Mosque

The **Al Abrar Mosque** ⓫ (daily 5–7am and 11.30am–9pm) is a few doors down. Built in the mid-1850s by the Indian Chulia community, it replaced the thatched hut that was established on the same site in 1827. Further along is the **Amoy Street Food Centre**, see ❸.

Telok Ayer Methodist Church

Follow the curve of the road. The 1925 **Telok Ayer Chinese Methodist Church** ⓬ (www.tacmc.org.sg; Mon–Fri 9am–5pm, Sat until 1pm), on your left, combines Chinese and Western elements such as Art Deco windows and European-style columns.

RED DOT DESIGN MUSEUM

Go through the Telok Ayer Park and cross Maxwell Road to the **red dot Traffic** building. Built in 1928, it housed the Traffic Police headquarters before it was refurbished and painted a striking red. It is now occupied by advertising agencies, a few bars, a café and the **red dot design museum** ⓭ (www.museum.red-dot.sg; Mon–Tue, Fri 11am–6pm, Sat–Sun until 8pm). Run by the German body that presents the prestigious red dot design awards, the museum has exhibitions of slick product designs from around the world. Worth checking out at red dot Traf-

fic is MAAD or Market of Artists & Designers (www.maad.sg; 1st weekend of every month 11am–8pm), a unique, curated bazaar showcasing work by local emerging artists and designers.

Exit the museum and turn right on Maxwell Road. The underground Tanjong Pagar MRT station is on the right after Wallich Street.

Food and drink

❶ MOLLY MALONE'S

56 Circular Road; tel: 6536 2029; www.molly-malone.com; Mon 11am–midnight, Tue–Sat 11am–2am; $$

At this Irish pub, enjoy excellent pub grub, such as fish and chips, shepherd's pie and Irish lamb stew.

❷ YAKUN

01-01 Far East Square; tel: 6438 3638; www.yakun.com; Mon–Fri 7.30am–6.30pm, Sat–Sun 8.30am–5pm; $

Established in 1944, Yakun serves a unique Singapore-style breakfast or teatime snack of soft-boiled eggs and kaya toast (grilled bread with coconut jam and butter).

❸ AMOY STREET FOOD CENTRE

Corner of Telok Ayer and Amoy streets; $

Great for local fare such as minced-meat noodles (noodles tossed with a chilli-vinegar sauce and topped with minced pork) and *char kway teow* (fried rice noodles with cockles).

Autumn festival lights

CHINATOWN

Like the city's other ethnic enclaves, Chinatown appeals with its fascinating blend of cultures. Visit a mosque, Hindu shrine and Buddhist temple, and explore its intriguing narrow streets, traditional shops and market stalls.

DISTANCE: 1.5km (1 mile)
TIME: Half a day
START: Jamae Mosque
END: Singapore City Gallery
POINTS TO NOTE: Take a taxi to Jamae Mosque at the corner of Mosque Street and South Bridge Road. Alternatively, take the MRT to the Chinatown station. The mosque is a short walk away.

It seems odd that Singapore, with a majority Chinese population, has a Chinatown. The neighbourhood only came to be known by this name as a result of the tourism board's efforts to promote the city's ethnic enclaves, although it has existed since the early days, when Chinese immigrants congregated south of the Singapore River.

Today's Chinatown is hemmed in by the soaring high-rises of the CBD, but vestiges of the traditional can still be seen. Conservation shophouses hold decades-old businesses, which stand shoulder to shoulder with even older places of worship. Medical halls dispense herbal cures, and exotic sights and smells, from rare Asian ingredients in the fresh-produce market to the pungent aroma of the durian fruit, still dominate the area.

JAMAE MOSQUE

Chinatown has its share of Chinese temples, but it also has some of the most well-known places of worship of other faiths. This walk starts on South Bridge Road at the **Jamae Mosque** ❶ (daily 9.30am–6pm). Built in 1826 by Tamil Muslims, it sports an eclectic mix of architectural styles, with pagoda-like minarets, a South India-style entrance gate and neoclassical prayer halls.

SRI MARIAMMAN TEMPLE

Cross Pagoda Street to the **Sri Mariamman Temple** ❷ (daily 7am–noon and 6–9pm). The temple was built in 1827 by Naraina Pillai, who accompanied Raffles on his second visit to Singapore in 1819. Dedicated to the goddess Mariamman, known for curing serious illnesses, it has a *gopuram* (tower),

Roof details of the Sri Mariamman Temple

adorned with vivid renditions of Hindu deities, at the entrance. If you happen to be here on the holy days of Tuesday and Friday, you can see brightly clad devotees offering *puja* (prayers). This temple is the site of the celebrations for Theemithi, the annual fire-walking festival that takes place around October or November.

Across South Bridge Road from Sri Mariamman Temple is **Eu Yan Sang**, a traditional Chinese medicine business that dates back to 1879. 'Eu' is the name of the family that founded it, and 'Yan Sang' means 'caring for mankind' in Cantonese. The shop stocks over 1,000 types of Chinese herbs and medicinal products, some of which, like herbal candies and bottled bird's-nest soup, make interesting souvenirs.

CHINATOWN HERITAGE CENTRE

Walk down **Pagoda Street**. Tucked among the many brightly coloured shophouses, at no.48, is the **Chinatown Heritage Centre** ❸ (www.singaporechinatown.com.sg; daily 9am–8pm). Using authentic furniture, utensils and other paraphernalia, the museum brings to life the harsh living conditions of Chinatown residents in the early years.

TRENGGANU AND SMITH STREETS

Turn right on New Bridge Road and then right again onto **Mosque Street. Togi**, see ❶, serves great Korean dishes and steamboat (hotpot). After your meal, retrace your steps, past Pagoda Street, and turn left onto Temple Street. You then come to the junction with **Trengganu Street** ❹, previously an opera street

Shopping for Chinese New Year decoration ornaments

with theatre stages and brothels. Today, you will find over 200 stalls at the Chinatown Street Market (daily 10am-10pm), sprawling over Trengganu, Pagoda, and Sago streets, which are all fully pedestrianised. Here you can pick up trinkets, tourist souvenirs and traditional Chinese goods like calligraphy and masks. In the days leading up to Chinese New Year, this whole area teems with stalls selling festive goodies, mandarin oranges and auspicious decorations.

Turn right onto Trengganu Street. At the corner with Smith Street is **Chinatown Complex ⑤**. This is perhaps one of the best places to catch glimpses of local life. At its basement, market vendors sell all manner of fresh produce and dried goods. Upstairs is a food centre with plenty of stalls dishing up excellent, old-fashioned hawker fare.

Diagonally opposite Chinatown Complex on Trengganu Street is **Lai Chun Yuen ⑥**, a former Chinese opera house dating back to the 1920s. This is one of the earliest three-storey buildings in the area, with a verandah running around the top level. It is now a budget hotel.

Further along **Smith Street** is the **Chinese Opera Teahouse ⑦** (no. 5; tel: 6323 4862; www.ctcopera.com.sg; Tue–Sun noon–5pm). Here you can have tea and snacks at traditional Chinese tables, surrounded by displays of opera costumes. On Friday and Saturday from 7pm to 9pm, you can enjoy dinner here while you watch Cantonese opera excerpts (booking advised).

Chinatown Food Street

Street hawkers have made a comeback at the open-air **Chinatown Food Street ⑧** (http://chinatownfoodstreet.sg; daily 11am–11pm) along Smith Street. Have a bite if hunger pangs strike or return here in the evening to sample local staples like *char kway teow* (fried flat rice noodles) and fish ball noodles. The high-ceiling glass canopy shelter and internal spot cooling system offers comfortable dining whether rain or shine.

SAGO STREET

Walk down Smith Street and turn right on South Bridge Road. A few steps away is **Sago Street ⑨**. Named after the numerous sago factories that operated here in the 1840s, the street was also a red-light district in the early 20th century. Today it is a pedestrian-only lane flanked by shophouses housing old-style Chinese medical halls and pastry shops on one side and souvenir and clothing stalls on the other. For a Western-style snack, try Austrian-style sausages at **Erich's Wuerstelstand**, see ❷, further down from Sago Street and Sago Lane.

BUDDHA TOOTH RELIC TEMPLE

Sandwiched between Sago Street and Sago Lane is the **Buddha Tooth Relic Temple and Museum ⑩** (www.btrts.org.sg; daily 7am–7pm; free). Its architecture, interiors and statuary are inspired by the styles of the Tang dynasty – a

Buddha Tooth Relic Temple

The temple contrasting with the CBD

golden age for Buddhism in China. The temple's centrepiece is one of the Buddha's sacred teeth, an object dogged by much controversy; its authenticity has been doubted by Buddhism scholars. It is held on the fourth floor in a golden stupa and only taken out for viewing on Vesak Day and Chinese New Year. More than half of the 420kg (930lbs) of gold needed to construct the stupa was donated by devotees. It is unveiled for viewing two times a day (9am and 3pm).

Entering the 80m (260ft) -high **100 Dragons Hall** on the ground level, you see an intricately carved 5m (20ft) -tall Maitreya Buddha image. A hundred other Buddha statues line the hall. On the third floor is the climate-controlled **Buddhist Culture Museum** (daily 8am–6pm), with precious Buddha images collected from all over Asia. On the roof you can admire the *Dendrobium Buddha Tooth*, an orchid hybrid named after the temple, and turn the huge prayer wheel in the **Ten Thousand Buddha Pavilion**.

SINGAPORE CITY GALLERY

After your temple visit, cross South Bridge Road to the **Maxwell Food Centre**, see ③, for some refreshments before continuing along Maxwell Road to the **Singapore City Gallery** ⑪ (www.ura.gov.sg/gallery; Mon–Sat 9am–5pm; free) at the URA Centre. The gallery's highlight is an enormous scaled and detailed 11x11m (36x36ft) architectural model of Singapore's central area. The rest of the gallery's 50 exhibits are spread over two storeys, including a multimedia exhibit that charts Singapore's architectural development over the past 180 years. You can also survey the vision planners have for the island in the 21st century.

Food and drink

① TOGI
11 Mosque Street; tel: 6221 0830; Mon–Sat noon–2pm, 6–9pm; $$
Located in a narrow shophouse, Togi serves homey Korean fare including comforting chicken ginseng soup, spicy tofu seafood soup and steamboat (hotpot) as well as other Korean favourites

② ERICH'S WUERSTELSTAND
Blk 5 Banda Street, 01-52 Stall No.5, K88 Coffee House; tel: 9627 4081; daily 11am–9pm; $
This stall is run by an Austrian chef who has lived in Asia for two decades. His grilled sausages include the traditional bratwurst and the boiled bockwurst served in a crispy roll topped with mustard.

③ MAXWELL FOOD CENTRE
Corner of South Bridge Road and Maxwell Road; daily 7am–10pm; $
This bustling food centre is a great place for dining round the clock from breakfast through to supper. Stalls that often have a queue are Zhen Zhen (no. 54) for its congee and Tian Tian (no. 10) for its chicken rice.

ORCHARD ROAD

No visit to Singapore is complete without a day's work on its most famous shopping artery, dense with ritzy malls and sidewalk cafés. The strip also has an enclave with exquisite Chinese Baroque–style houses.

DISTANCE: 3km (2 miles), not including the distances covered in the malls
TIME: A full day
START: Tanglin Mall
END: MacDonald House
POINTS TO NOTE: To get to Tanglin Mall, at the corner of Tanglin and Grange roads, take a taxi or bus no. 36, which stops in front of The Regent hotel. Most shops and malls open at 10.30 or 11am and close at 9 or 10pm.

The famous Orchard Road was so named because of the many nutmeg, pepper and fruit plantations found here in the 1800s. In the 1840s the area was also dotted with cemeteries. But by the 20th century, Orchard metamorphosed into a vibrant commercial centre and later into the city's flashiest shopping address and style headquarters, teeming with malls and luxury hotels. The city's passion for shopping is easily demonstrated by the numerous, overcrowded malls on Orchard Road. It would be too exhaust-ing to visit all the malls in a day; this tour guides you to the shopping highlights and a few historical sights, starting from the Tanglin area.

TANGLIN ROAD

Begin with a fortifying brunch at **Caffe Beviamo**, see ❶, in **Tanglin Mall ❶**, which has boutiques and gourmet-food shops.

From Tanglin Mall, walk up Tanglin Road to **Tudor Court ❷**. If you are inter-ested in Asian artefacts and antiques, a few of the shops here are worth a browse. The upscale French gourmet store Hédiard is also here, with caviar, wines, preserves, teas and spices. Con-tinue past **St Regis Hotel** and on to **Tanglin Shopping Centre ❸**. The latter's dated exterior belies the quality antiques and art found in its galleries and shops.

FORUM, HILTON AND FOUR SEASONS

Follow the bend around Orchard Parade Hotel into Orchard Road proper. On the

Orchard Road, packed with shoppers

right is **Forum The Shopping Mall** ❹, filled with boutiques for children and mothers.

Further on from Forum, look out for the two Chinese warrior statues in front of the **Hilton Hotel** ❺. These 'doorway guardians' are said to offer protection from evil spirits. The Shopping Gallery Hilton Singapore is a good stop for designer jewellery and haute couture in the likes of Issey Miyake and Lanvin.

It also connects to the **Four Seasons Hotel's shopping arcade** just behind. The **Club 21** gallery here features Balenciaga, Mulberry, Marc Jacobs and other luxe fashion labels.

Palais Renaissance and around

Opposite the Hilton is the swanky **Palais Renaissance** ❻, with a few boutiques and Passion Hair Salon frequented by local celebrities and well-heeled ladies.

When King Chulalongkorn visited Singapore in the 1890s, he bought the property next to Palais Renaissance. Today, this is the Thai Embassy (www.thaiembassy.sg). It hosts an annual Thai Festival in its spacious garden in June, during which you can catch a whiff of pungent durians even from a distance.

On the opposite side, after the ageing Far East Shopping Centre, is **Liat Towers** ❼, which hosts Spanish brands Zara and Massimo Dutti as well as luxury label Hermès. Beside it is **Wheelock Place** ❽, designed by Japanese superstar architect Kisho Kurokawa. Its glass pyramid is a landmark. Marks & Spencer

and a variety of speciality shops and eateries can be found here.

SCOTTS ROAD

Cross the road to **Shaw Centre** ❾, home to the Japanese department store Isetan, as well as Lido Cineplex, which underwent a major refurbishment and now houses 11 cinemas including Singapore's first and only IMAX's Digital Theatre System.

Further on Scotts Road, past Royal Plaza on Scotts hotel, is the striking red **DFS Galleria** ❿, which stocks a wide variety of duty-free goods, from high-end clothing to kitschy souvenirs.

Far East Plaza

Take the overhead bridge to the **Far East Plaza** ⓫. Its eclectic hole-in-the-wall shops target teens looking for affordable streetwear but there is also no lack of bespoke tailors, tattoo parlours and karaoke pubs. Though the building has not worn its years well, it is still a great place for bargains.

Goodwood Park Hotel

Far East Plaza is sandwiched between **Goodwood Park Hotel** ⓬ and the Grand Hyatt. Designed by Swan and MacLaren after the castles along the River Rhine, the Goodwood Park was originally built as the Teutonia Club in 1900 for the German community.

During World War I, the club was seized as an enemy property and then

Goodwood Park

auctioned off to three Jewish brothers who turned it into a performance venue, christened Goodwood Hall. One of its highlights in 1922 was a performance by one of the world's greatest ballerinas, Anna Pavlova.

In 1929 the hall was converted into a hotel. The Japanese used it as their military headquarters during their occupation, and in 1945 the British turned it into a war-crimes court. Its Grand Tower, which became a national monument in 1989, has notable architectural elements such as fluted columns, delicate woodwork and graceful archways.

On the other side of Far East Plaza is the **Grand Hyatt** ⑱, which has angled doors and a Zen-inspired fountain in its lobby. These features reportedly were designed to address *feng shui* concerns; the hotel's business is said to have boomed after they were installed.

THE MAIN STRETCH

At the junction of Scotts and Orchard roads is the pagoda-like **Marriott Hotel** ⑭. Adjoining it is **TANGS** department store, noted for its cult skincare brands and kitchen gadgets. TANGS was founded by C.K. Tang, who arrived in Singapore from China in 1922. He made his fortune peddling China-made lace from house to house. Among the first to recognise the potential of Orchard Road, the Christian was unperturbed by the presence of a Chinese cemetery opposite the store's location. In fact, business flour-

ished and outgrew the original smaller building. Next door is **Lucky Plaza** ⑮. It is tatty around the edges but still popular for bargain electronic goods.

Situated opposite TANGS is **ION Orchard** ⑯. This swanky mall houses flagship stores of numerous luxury brands such as Prada, Miu Miu and Marc Jacobs, as well as many food outlets. Head up to IONSKY at the 56th floor, the highest point on Orchard Road, for 360-degree views of Singapore through special telescopes.

Next to ION is the Orchard MRT station. Further on is the fashion-centred **Wisma Atria** ⑰, with a branch of the Japanese department store Isetan and numerous high-street fashion boutiques. A good

Find information here

Futuristic ION Orchard mall

lunch spot here is **Food Republic**, see ②.

Linked by an underpass to Wisma Atria is the oversized **Ngee Ann City** ⑱ with boutiques selling everything from haute couture to street fashion. Its anchor tenant, **Takashimaya** department store, has a wonderful food hall, purveying delicacies from the world over, including England's Harrods and many fine Japanese brands. **Books Kinokuniya** on the fourth floor stocks all manner of books and magazines. On the same floor, there are a few art galleries and stylish stationers.

Unbridled consumerism continues across the road in **The Paragon** ⑲, filled with boutiques of top international designer names such as Gucci, Prada, Salvatore Ferragamo and Tod's. Also

located here are Marks & Spencer, Toys 'R' Us and a good range of eateries.

Opposite The Paragon is Grand Park Orchard Hotels's Knightsbridge, housing retail stores such as Abercrombie & Fitch and Tommy Hilfiger. Further along is **Robinsons Orchard** ⑳ which has taken over the entire Heeren building and filled it with all manner of mid to high-end fashion, beauty, home and lifestyle brands.

Opposite The Heeren is Meritus Mandarin Hotel and its stylish shopping arcade, **Mandarin Gallery** ㉑. There are various well-known boutiques here including one by local designer Ashley Isham. Food-wise, there are several good outlets such as the famous **Ippudo SG** ramen eaterie from Japan, see ③.

Signage at Centrepoint

Tourist information

Swing by the **Singapore Visitors Centre** ㉒ (daily 9.30am–10.30pm), at the junction of Cairnhill and Orchard roads, where you can get information on sights, book tours and purchase tickets to events.

EMERALD HILL

The Somerset MRT station is close by, if you want to call it a day. Opposite the station is **Peranakan Place** ㉓, a complex of highly ornamented Straits Chinese terrace houses. At its shaded terrace café, relax with a drink. Then explore the lovely Chinese Baroque-style terrace houses further up the slope, on **Emerald Hill** ㉔.

The 30 double-storey terrace houses on Emerald Hill, built between 1901 and 1925, have thankfully not been razed but carefully restored, having been accorded conservation status in the 1980s, which means their owners are not allowed to alter their facades.

Today, although the interiors of most of these houses have been refurbished, their original facades remain well-preserved. Look out for ceramic tiles with flower motifs, ornamental mouldings, and carved swing doors. Check out no. 83 for its original facade with pastel blue wood, and no. 73, which has intricate gold paintwork on its wooden shutters. The value of these houses is sky-high, and many are rented out to well-heeled expatriates. You may be able to peek inside some of these plush homes if the doors are ajar.

There are also a few watering holes on Emerald Hill. Establishments such as **No. 5** (tel: 6732 0818), **Ice Cold Beer** (see page 122) and the atmospheric **Alley Bar** (see page 122) are long-standing favourites. **Que Pasa**, see ❹, is great for tapas and sangria.

CENTREPOINT

If you still have the time and energy for more shopping, step into one of the older but popular malls **Centrepoint** ㉕. Taking over the former **Robinsons** space is Metro departmental store which will boast six levels of fashion and lifestyle products.

Orchard Central

Opposite Centrepoint is **Orchard Central** ㉖, a retail development dedicated

---

The Istana

The Istana (www.istana.gov.sg) ('palace' in Malay) is the office and official residence of Singapore's president, Tony Tan. Built in 1869, the elegant neo-Palladian Anglo-Indian building was once the British governor's residence. During the Japanese occupation, it was used by Japanese army commanders. The grounds of the Istana are open to the public from 8.30am to 6pm on Labour Day, Hari Raya Puasa, National Day, Deepavali and Chinese New Year. Foreigners need to pay a $1 entrance fee. On the first Sunday of every month, a changing-of-guards ceremony takes place at the main gate from 5.45pm.

House on Emerald Hill   *A wealth of brands*

to Asian brands. The Orchard Central site has an interesting history. In the 1970s it was Glutton's Square, a popular open-air street-dining spot. The food stalls were revived during the 2004 Singapore Food Festival but have since been relocated next to The Esplanade and renamed Makansutra Gluttons Bay.

Adjacent to Orchard Central is **orchardgateway** ㉗, the only mall that straddles both sides of Orchard Road. High-street fashion brands, indie fashion stores and blogshops are found here. Next door is **313 Somerset** ㉘ which has a massive Food Republic Food Court. Somerset MRT is just below this mall.

DHOBY GHAUT

A 10-minute walk from Centrepoint, past the drab Orchard Plaza and Concorde Hotel takes you to the gate of the **Istana** ㉙, the Singapore president's official residence. Opposite is the leafy **Istana Park** ㉚, with pretty landscaping. Its centrepiece is the Festival Arch, a structure with banners, flags and a design that echoes the Istana entrance.

Beside the Istana is yet another mall, **Plaza Singapura** ㉛, with Golden Village cinemas and Japan's two-dollar store, Daiso. Next door is **The Atrium@ Orchard** ㉜, linked to the Dhoby Ghaut MRT station by an underpass.

MacDonald House ㉝, one of the oldest multistorey office buildings in this area, stands next to The Atrium, marking the end of Orchard Road.

Food and drink

① CAFFE BEVIAMO
02-K1 Tanglin Mall, 163 Tanglin Road; tel: 6738 7906; daily 9am–9pm; $$
Generously portioned sandwiches, salads, antipasti and pastas. Order the sticky date pudding sandwich with vanilla ice cream.

② FOOD REPUBLIC
04-00 Wisma Atria; tel: 6737 9881; Mon–Thu and Sun 10am–10pm, Fri–Sat until 11pm; $
This massive food court's décor is reminiscent of the hawker set-ups of yesteryear. Retro-looking pushcarts offer dim sum and drinks, while a huge variety of stalls sell local food.

③ IPPUDO SG
04-02/03/04 Mandarin Gallery, 333A Orchard Road; tel: 6235 2797; www.ippudo.com.sg; Mon–Sat 11am–11pm, Sun 11am–10pm; $$
This famous ramen eatery from Japan sees long queues at meal times, so get there early. Slurp up the famed authentic ramen in a creamy tonkotse broth brewed for over 20 hours.

④ QUE PASA
7 Emerald Hill Road; tel: 6235 6626; www.emeraldhillgroup.com; daily noon–2am; $$
Located in a Peranakan townhouse, this Spanish-inspired bar serves sangria and a range of wines as well as delicious tapas.

Orchid blooms

BOTANIC GARDENS AND TANGLIN VILLAGE

The Botanic Gardens, a lovely green lung minutes away from Orchard Road, offers luxuriant trees, virgin jungle and a fabulous orchid garden. Close by, find Tanglin Village, with stylish restaurants and antiques shops.

DISTANCE: 3.5km (2 miles)
TIME: 3–4 hours
START: Botanic Gardens
END: Tanglin Village
POINTS TO NOTE: Do this walk in the early morning or late afternoon when the air is fresher and the weather cooler. The main Tanglin Gate entrance to the Botanic Gardens is at the junction of Holland and Napier roads. This walk starts the Central Core, accessed via the Nassim Gate entrance on Cluny Road. The nearest MRT station is Orchard. From there, take a taxi to the Visitor Centre at the junction of Nassim and Cluny roads.

The first botanic garden in Singapore was established in 1822 on Fort Canning Hill by Stamford Raffles as an experimental station for commercial cultivation. Its most notable crop was the Pará rubber tree (*Hevea brasiliensis*), from Brazil, introduced by Henry Ridley, who went on to establish Malaya's rubber industry.

BOTANIC GARDENS

The present 64-hectare (158-acre) **Singapore Botanic Gardens** (www.sbg.org.sg; daily 5am–midnight; free) was founded by an agri-horticultural society in 1859 and subsequently handed over to the colonial administration for maintenance. Today the gardens contain over 3,000 species of trees and shrubs, in areas as varied as virgin jungle, marshland, lakes and formal gardens. It is also a centre for horticultural and botanical research and experimentation, with an emphasis on orchid breeding and hybridisation.

Before you begin your walk, get a bite at **Casa Verde**, see ❶, at the **Visitor Centre ❶**. After your meal, go through the Palm Court, with cascading water features and palm trees, veer right and walk towards the Evolution Garden.

Evolution Garden

The **Evolution Garden ❷** (daily 5am–7pm) is a cleverly designed garden, with landscaping that chronicles the evolution of plants from the pre-historic times till the present day. Rock formations are interspersed among ferns and trees that are rarely found on the streets of modern cities. Look out for the curious-looking giant club-mosses, the prehistoric equivalent of trees today, and stone columns of 'petrified' tree trunks, which are fossilised remains of ancient trees.

Leave the Evolution Garden and retrace your steps to the Palm Court and past a 1920s black-and-white colonial bungalow, home to the fine-dining **Corner House**. Continue on Heliconia Walk. From here you can see the **Shaw Foundation Symphony Stage ❸**, flanked by the **Symphony Lake** and the rolling lawns of the **Palm Valley**, which teem with picnickers during weekend concerts.

National Orchid Garden

Head down Upper Palm Valley Road to the **National Orchid Garden ❹** (daily 8.30am–7pm; charge), whose landscaped grounds are filled with a profusion of gorgeous orchids. It has the largest orchid display in the world with some 1,000 species and 2,000 hybrids, and more are added every year. The meandering paths and fountains make this a charming walk.

Water features complement the lush greenery

Highlights include the **VIP Orchid Garden**, with hybrids named after state dignitaries and VIPs, such as Paravanda Nelson Mandela and Vanda William Catherine. Look out for the *Vanda Miss Joaquim*. This hybrid was discovered by Agnes Joaquim in her garden in 1893 and was selected as Singapore's national flower in 1981 because of its hardiness and resilience. Next to the VIP Orchid Garden is **Burkill Hall**, a colonial plantation bungalow built in 1886. It is now used to showcase information on the different hybrids named after the VIPs who have visited the garden. Don't miss the **Cool House**, a simulated tropical montane forest habitat, draped with orchids, epiphytes and carnivorous pitcher plants.

Ginger Garden

Continue to the **Ginger Garden** ❺ to see a collection of flora from the ginger family, including bananas and heliconias. The restaurant **Halia**, see ❷, is located here.

Lower Ring Road

Take the Lower Ring Road, along which you will come across a white cast-iron **bandstand**, built in 1930.

Further down Lower Ring Road are a series of **bronze sculptures** by Sydney Harpley: *Girl on a Swing, Girl on a Bicycle and Lady on a Hammock*. Completed 1984–1989 and symbolising freedom and exuberance, they were gifted by David Marshall, Singapore's first chief minister, and are dedicated to the children of Singapore.

Swan Lake

Turn right when you come to the **Swiss Granite Fountain** and walk past the **Sundial Garden** to **Swan Lake** ❻, with a huge swan sculpture in its heart. Visitors, especially families with children, come here to feed the few swans and terrapins.

The path then brings you to the Tanglin Gate; exit the gardens here.

TANGLIN VILLAGE

After your Botanic Gardens tour, hop in a taxi to **Tanglin Village** (Dempsey Hill; www.dempseyhill.com), located off Holland Road (only about five minutes away), for lunch or dinner.

Originally a nutmeg plantation, the area was converted to the Tanglin Barracks, occupied by British troops in the 1860s and later abandoned. In recent years, the barracks have been given a new lease of life and are now a thriving lifestyle and dining destination, organised into three clusters: Dempsey, Minden and Loewen.

Dempsey Cluster

The **Dempsey Cluster** ❼ is the most developed, with plenty of good restaurants and stores selling Asian-style furniture, artefacts and antiques amid lush greenery. A favourite among locals is the durian stall located at the car park. You can catch scents of the pungent fruit a distance away.

If you need a rub down to soothe your muscles after your walk, book one at Spa Esprit at **Beauty Emporium** (02-01, 8D

Strolling in the serene gardens

Dempsey Road; tel: 6479 0070; daily 10am–9pm), where the menu includes facials, massages and foot spas.

The Dempsey cluster offers a carefully curated selection of restaurants. Recommended are **Jones the Grocer**, see ❸, **Samy's Curry**, see ❹ **Long Beach Seafood**, see ❺, and **Road House**, see ❻.

Minden Cluster

The **Minden Cluster** ❽ is home to the Tanglin Golf Course and the Anglican **St George's Church** (www.stgeorges.org.sg), built in 1911 as a garrison church for British troops. This pretty red-brick building, in classical Romanesque style, was made a national monument in 1978.

Food and drink

❶ CASA VERDE

Visitors Centre Singapore Botanic Gardens; tel: 6467 7326; www.lesamis.com.sg; daily 7.30–11am, noon–6pm, 6.30–11pm; $$

This alfresco spot is managed by the Les Amis Group. It serves both local and Italian cuisine. Breakfast and an all-day dining menu including wood-fired pizzas are also available.

❷ HALIA

Ginger Garden, Botanic Gardens; tel:6287 0711; www.thehalia.com; Mon–Fri noon–4pm, Mon–Thu 6.30–9.30pm, Fri–Sat 6.30–10pm, Sun 5.30pm–9.30pm; $$–$$$
Halia ('ginger' in Malay) is nestled amid lush tropical foliage. The all-day menu features modern European fare with Asian flavours.

❸ JONES THE GROCER

01-12, Blk 9 Dempsey Road; tel: 6476 1512; www.jonesthegrocer.com; daily 9am–11pm; $$
This Australian gourmet store with a café is a

great place for a coffee and a sweet treat or a light lunch.

❹ SAMY'S CURRY

25 Dempsey Road; tel: 6472 2080; www.samyscurry.com; Mon, Wed–Sun 11am–3pm and 6–10pm, $$
Delicious South Indian fare is served on banana leaves. Samy's has a faithful following for its fish-head curry.

❺ LONG BEACH SEAFOOD

01-01, 25 Dempsey Road; tel: 6323 2222; www.longbeachseafood.com.sg; daily 11am–3pm and 5.30pm–1am; $$$
Excellent Singapore-style seafood dishes, including black pepper crab, chilli crab and fried baby squid.

❻ ROAD HOUSE

13 Dempsey Road; tel: 6476 2922; Mon–Fri 11.30am–3.30pm, 6.30–11pm, Sat–Sun 9am–11pm; $$
This modern American 'diner' rolls out substantial burgers, grilled steaks, spare ribs and one-of-a-kind desserts (think: warm salted triple nut pie).

Shophouses on Arab Street

KAMPONG GLAM

The Arab Quarter has shed its sleepy image with the entry of stylish boutiques and cafés, but its Malay and Middle Eastern essence can still be felt in the dignified mosques and traditional businesses.

DISTANCE: 1.5km (1 mile)
TIME: 3–4 hours
START: Arab Street
END: Bali Lane
POINTS TO NOTE: This is recommended as a late-morning-to-afternoon walk as many of the shops only open for business in the afternoon. Take a taxi to Arab Street or the MRT to the Bugis station and walk for 15 minutes to the starting point.

The enclave's name means 'village of the *gelam* tree'. The tree's bark was prized for its medicinal value and used by the early Bugis and Malay residents to caulk boats, although it would be difficult to find this tree here now.

This neighbourhood used to run along the shore, with many of its houses built on stilts above the tidal mudflats. Much of Kampong Glam was mangrove swamp and was drained in the 1820s. Beach Road, as its name suggests, was

Stamford Raffles allocated this area to Sultan Hussein, the Malay king who ceded the island to the British in 1824. The sultan built a palace here for his family and homes for his retainers. Subsequently Javanese and Minangkabau traders, Arab textile merchants and even Chinese tombstone makers settled here, alongside the Malay community.

Rishi Handicrafts' caneware

once a coastal road. In the 1880s reclamation pushed the road further inland.

Today's Kampong Glam extends over the area bordered by Ophir Road, Victoria Street, Jalan Sultan and Beach Road. Its main landmarks are centuries-old mosques, but lately, it has also drawn a new following with local designer boutiques, cafés and restaurants.

ARAB STREET

Start your stroll on **Arab Street ❶**. These shops and eateries here are set in restored two-storey shophouses, many of which were built in the Early Shophouse style in the 1840s, resembling unadorned dollhouses with their squat upper levels and simple lines.

Along Arab Street are shops selling ethnic jewellery, alcohol-free perfumes and all manner of fabrics. At the corner of Arab and Baghdad streets is **Rishi Handicrafts** (no. 58), its shopfront displaying baskets and other caneware. Opposite Rishi is **Goodwill Trading** (no. 56), its walls covered with batiks. There are also several shops along this street selling Oriental carpets. For a quick bite, try **Café Le Caire**, see ❶.

BUSSORAH STREET

Turn left on Beach Road and pass the fishing tackle shops. Turn left again, onto the narrow **Bussorah Street ❷**, lined with eateries and souvenir shops. The British named Bussorah Street after an

Iraqi town to commemorate their victory against the Turks in World War I. During the Ramadan fasting month before the Muslim celebration of Hari Raya Puasa each year, this street bustles with food vendors and their Muslim customers, who buy home-cooked delicacies for breaking their fast at sunset. On the right is **Amirah's Grill**, see ❷, serving Middle Eastern cuisine.

Further along at no. 21 is a Malay food stall that has been in business without a name on its signage for more than three decades. Many locals come for its *teh tarik* ('pulled' tea), *nasi lemak* (rice cooked in coconut milk), *pisang goreng* (banana fritters) and Malay cakes.

Past the Bussorah Street junction is **Bussorah Mall**, a quiet pedestrianised street flanked by restored 19th-century shophouses. Sultan Mosque looms at the end of the street.

SULTAN MOSQUE

Sultan Mosque ❸ (www.sultanmosque. org.sg; Mon–Thu, Sat–Sun 9.30am–noon, 2–4pm, Fri 9.30am–noon and 2.30–4pm), distinguished by its golden onion dome and soaring minarets, is the most important place of Muslim worship in Singapore. The first mosque on this site was built in 1824 by Sultan Hussein. The current structure, the largest mosque in Singapore with a 5,000-capacity prayer hall, was completed in 1928. The colonial architect firm Swan and Maclaren adopted the design of the Taj Mahal in

Relaxing at a café

India and combined it with Persian, Moorish, Turkish and classical themes.

MALAY HERITAGE CENTRE

Leave the mosque and turn left onto Kandahar Street, where you will find the **Istana Kampong Gelam**, set in a beautiful garden (Tue–Sun 8am–8pm, Fri–Sat 8am–10pm; free). Its architecture combines traditional Malay motifs with a Palladian style that dates back to the 1840s.

The **Malay Heritage Centre** ❹ (www. malayheritage.org.sg; Tue–Sun 10am–6pm) is housed in the Istana building and has six permanent galleries showcasing interesting regalia of the Malay royalty and artefacts pertaining to Malay history and culture. The adjacent two-storey **Gedung Kuning** ('Yellow Mansion'), originally built for Tengku Mahmoud, grandson of Sultan Hussein, was bought over in 1912 by Haji Yusoff, a Malay entrepreneur and philanthropist in Singapore. His family owned Gedung Kuning until 1999 when the Singapore government acquired the building.

KANDAHAR STREET

Walk down **Kandahar Street** ❺ towards North Bridge Road. Kandahar Street is named after the city in Afghanistan, originally part of the British empire. The old shophouses here have been accorded conservation status. Their architecture is a fusion of European, Malay, Chinese and Indian elements. Look out for the units with swinging doors known as *pintu pagar*.

If you have not had lunch, cross North Bridge Road and turn left towards **Jalan Pisang**. At no. 11 on this street is the **Hajjah Maimunah Restaurant**, see ❸. Further down on North Bridge Road is **Zam Zam** ❹, a local institution.

HAJI LANE

Continue on North Bridge Road, go past Arab Street and turn onto **Haji Lane** ❻. Here you will find some seriously hip

---

Historical mosques

Apart from the grand Sultan Mosque, there are two other mosques in the Arab Quarter that make worthy detours. At the corner of Jalan Sultan and Victoria Street you'll see the golden domes of the blue mosaic-tiled **Malabar Muslim Jama-Ath Mosque** (daily 10am–noon and 2–4pm). The mosque, established by Indian Muslims from the Malabar coast of Kerala, harks back to the time Kampong Glam was founded. Behind Jalan Sultan and off Beach Road is **Hajjah Fatimah Mosque** (daily 9am–9pm), named after a Muslim shipping entrepreneur who donated her home to be the site of this mosque. Designed by a British architect, this European-style building, completed in 1846, features a stained-glass dome. Because its spire tilts at six degrees, the mosque is dubbed Singapore's 'Leaning Tower'.

Textiles for sale

boutiques that have been opened by young local designers, as well as vintage stores. Some of the best include **Dulcet Fig** (no. 41; http://dulcetfig.com; Mon–Thu 1–9pm, Fri–Sat until 10pm, Sun 2–6pm), which sells vintage clothing and quirky accessories, and **Salad** (no. 25/27 Mon–Sat noon–8pm), profering home and fashion accessories as well as clothes in mainly black and white colours.

BALI LANE

Take the small lane that leads from Haji Lane to **Bali Lane ❼**. Shoppers can continue to browse at **Threadbare & Squirrel** (660 North Bridge Road; daily 12.30–8.30pm), a boutique that sells a range of women's and men's clothing, as well as bags and shoes.

A nice end to your afternoon is **Blu Jaz Café** (no. 11; www.blujaz.net; Mon–Thu noon–midnight, Fri until 2am, Sat 4pm–2am), a casual restaurant-bar. Linger for a while or return in the evening to catch its live jazz performances.

To leave this area, cross Ophir Road, parallel to Bali Lane; the Bugis MRT station is just ahead.

Food and drink

❶ CAFÉ LE CAIRE

39 Arab Street; tel: 6292 0979; www.cafe lecaire.com; Sun–Thu 10am–3.30am, Fri–Sat 10am–5.30am ; $$

The dishes come in generous portions and are good for sharing. Try the mezze platter, falafel and kebabs. If you prefer to dine in air-conditioned comfort, head upstairs to the cosy dining room.

❷ AMIRAH'S GRILL

14 Bussorah Street; tel: 6344 1610; daily 11.30am-11.30pm; $$

This Middle Eastern and Mediterranean restaurant, helmed by an Egyptian chef, rolls out signature dishes such as Turkish grilled kofta served with Arabic rice. There are also Western dishes such as grilled beef ribs and lamb chops.

❸ HAJJAH MAIMUNAH RESTAURANT

11 &15 Jalan Pisang; tel: 6297 4294; www.hj maimunah.com; Mon–Sat 7am–8pm; $

This small, modest eatery has a fierce following so it is usually full. Join in the queue and make your choices at the counter. The spread includes tender beef *rendang* (dry curry) stewed in coconut milk, grilled chicken and colourful Malay cakes.

❹ SINGAPORE ZAM ZAM RESTAURANT

697–699 North Bridge Road; tel: 6298 6320; daily 8am–11pm; $

A popular spot serving Indian-Muslim specialties. Tuck into robustly spicy mutton or chicken biryani with aromatic basmati rice, as well as murtabak breads, stuffed with minced mutton or chicken.

LITTLE INDIA

Take a walk through the most characterful ethnic enclave in Singapore, to experience the heart of Singapore's Indian culture with all your senses; discover spirited daily life, heady aromas of spices and enchanting traditional rituals.

DISTANCE: 1.5km (1 mile)
TIME: 2–3 hours
START: Little India Arcade
END: Leong San See Temple
POINTS TO NOTE: Late morning is a good time to start this route. Take a taxi or the MRT to the Little India station, a short walk to the starting point.

Little India spreads over the area bounded by Sungei Road, Jalan Besar, Lavender Street and Race Course Road. **Serangoon Road** through its heart, a thoroughfare from which numerous backlanes, lined with small shops spilling over with saris, fabrics and floral garlands, fan out.

The enclave was designated by Stamford Raffles as the Indian district in his 1822 town plan, first thriving as a cattle-rearing ground. It later grew as a hub of Indian commerce, just as it still is today, although many of the traditional businesses have made way for contemporary ones. Little India is a magnet for both migrant workers and tourists from the Indian subcontinent.

BACKSTREETS

Begin your tour at the Art Deco-style **Little India Arcade ❶** and spend some time perusing the stalls selling crafts, jewellery and souvenirs. Exiting the mall, turn left on **Clive Street**, where little shops are crammed with cookware.

Turn left onto **Campbell Lane ❷**. In the arts and craft shops here, you can find a jumble of rugs, soft furnishings, trinkets, Christian icons and Buddha and Ganesh images. At **Jothi Store & Flower Shop** (no. 1; daily 9am–9pm), fragrant jasmine flowers are strung into garlands, to be offered in Hindu temples.

Turn right onto Serangoon Road, which is dotted with restaurants, some of them established since the time when the area was largely populated by single men, whose domestic arrangements did not include private kitchens. Stop by **Ananda Bhavan**, see ❶, for ginger tea and South Indian snacks.

From Serangoon Road, turn right onto **Dunlop Street ❸**. You can see a typical provision shop with interesting Asian fruits and vegetables, from bitter gourd

Sri Veeramakaliamman Temple.

to betel leaves, heaped into crates and baskets that spill over onto the walkway. Spices such as bright yellow turmeric, deep red saffron and mellow brown cinnamon, assail your senses with their aromas and colours.

Tucked away at 41 Dunlop Street is **Abdul Gafoor Mosque**, an Arabian- and Renaissance-style mosque (daily 7am–noon and 2.30–4.30pm), built in 1859. Its prayer hall is decorated with Moorish arches and has a tableau tracing the origins of Islam.

When you have seen enough of Dunlop Street, backtrack to Serangoon Road. This stretch of the thoroughfare contains shops selling multicoloured saris and accessories on both sides. Another Little India institution here is **Komala Vilas**, see ❷, offering good vegetarian food.

SRI VEERAMAKALIAMMAN TEMPLE

Across the street, past Belilios Road, stands the **Sri Veeramakaliamman Temple** ❹ (www.sriveeramakaliamman.com; daily 5.30am–12.30pm and 4–9pm), dating from 1835. It is dedicated to the multi-armed goddess Kali, the manifestation of anger against evil. As consort to Shiva, Kali is also known as Parvati in her benign form. Therefore she is both feared as well as loved. In the main shrine, her statue is flanked by those of her sons – Murugan, the child god, and Ganesh, the Elephant God.

The temple is packed with devotees on the Hindu holy days of Tuesday and Friday. They often break a coconut before entering to denote the breaking of their ego. Cracked shells are tossed into the aluminium receptacles under the *gopuram*

In Mustafa Centre

(tower). Fresh coconut and mango leaves above the entrance symbolise purity and welcome; the lotus represents human striving for spiritual perfection; and banana offerings indicate abundance.

ANGULLIA MOSQUE

Continue on Serangoon Road to Birch Road, with another historical place of worship, the **Angullia Mosque** ❺ (daily 4.30–8am and noon–10pm), built over 100 years ago. Cross over to the other side to Syed Alwi Road and visit the decidedly secular phenomenon that is **Mustafa Centre** ❻. Mustafa Centre (145 Syed Alwi Road; tel: 6295 5855; www.mustafa.com.sg; daily 24 hours) is a department store like no other in Singapore. Open around the clock, it stocks the widest selection of merchandise, from the latest power tools to the most obscure toiletries, heaped bazaar-style. The Mustafa success has spawned a hotel, café and travel agency, plus an extension of the mall on Verdun Road. The best time to shop here is the wee hours of the morning when the aisles are nearly empty, and the worst is Sunday, when it is really crowded.

Turn right onto **Kampong Kapur Road**, where the garish Royal India Hotel stands, and right again onto **Desker Road**. This street has plenty of cheap hotels and a seedy reputation. Turn right onto **Lembu Road**, where Indian migrant workers in the construction industry congregate on the Lembu Road Open Space.

SRI SRINIVASA PERUMAL TEMPLE

Turn left onto Syed Alwi Road and make your way to Serangoon Road. It is a good 10-minute walk to the next place of interest. After passing Fortuna Hotel and the Kitchener Road junction, cross to the opposite side. After Perumal Road is the brightly coloured **Sri Srinivasa Perumal Temple** ❼ (daily 6.30am–noon and 6–9pm). It was founded by migrant Naradimhaloo Naidu, who endowed a portion of his property to the temple in 1860. A century later, local philanthropist P. Govindasamy Pillay met the expenses for adding the five-tier *gopuram* (tower), which rises 21m (70ft) above the entrance. Figures on the *gopuram* depict the various incarnations of Vishnu, also known as Perumal, the Preserver of Life, who appears on Earth in different forms.

Thaipusam

Each year during Thaipusam, around January or February, a procession of devotees begins at the Sri Srinivasa Perumal Temple and ends at the Chettiar Temple on Tank Road. The men pierce their tongues, cheeks and bodies with skewers that support their *kavadi*, heavy arched steel structures decorated with peacock feathers. Women devotees participating in the procession carry jugs of milk on their heads. These acts of faith are performed either as penance or in gratitude to Lord Murugan, Shiva's son.

Jewellery boxes

Leave the temple and follow the adjacent path, past blocks of public housing and a tiny playground, to **Race Course Road**.

SAKYA MUNI BUDDHA GAYA TEMPLE

Little India may be the hub of the Hindu community, but, reflective of Singapore's multicultural nature, it also has places of worship of various faiths.

To your right is the **Sakya Muni Buddha Gaya Temple** ❽ (daily 8am–4.45pm), which is also known as the Temple of 1,000 Lights because the 15m (50-ft) -high statue of the seated Buddha is surrounded by a halo with that many light bulbs. Inside the door is part of a branch from the sacred bodhi tree under which the Buddha is said to have attained enlightenment. Worshippers may illuminate the lights around the statue for a small donation.

LEONG SAN SEE TEMPLE

Further down the road on your left are some lovely old houses and the **Leong San See Temple** ❾ (no. 371; daily 6am–6pm) with an ornately carved roof. The temple is dedicated to Guan Yin, the Goddess of Mercy. Its altar also has an image of Confucius; the temple is hence popular with parents who bring their children to pray for success in examinations.

Have a meal at one of the popular restaurants on Race Course Road, such as **Banana Leaf Apolo**, see ❸, before you call it a day. The Farrer Park MRT station is nearby.

Food and drink

❶ ANANDA BHAVAN

58 Serangoon Road; tel: 6297 9522; daily 7.30am–10.30pm; www.anandabhavan. com; $

Established in 1924, Ananda Bhavan serves South Indian vegetarian dishes, like crispy *thosai*, a pancake made of rice and gram flour, eaten with lentil gravy or filled with spicy potato curry.

❷ KOMALA VILAS

76–78 Serangoon Road; tel: 6293 6980; daily 7.30am–10:30pm; www.komalavilas.com.sg; $

This place is known for its cheap vegetarian Indian food and its many varieties of *thosai*. Fast-food style meals are served downstairs, and restaurant-style seating is available upstairs.

❸ BANANA LEAF APOLO

54–58 Race Course Road; tel: 6293 8682; www.bananaleafapolo.com; daily 10.30am–10.30pm; $$

The fish-head curry is a must-try, as is the mutton or chicken *biryani* (basmati rice cooked with spices), served on banana leaves. A range of North Indian dishes are available too.

SENTOSA

Sentosa, the largest of Singapore's offshore isles, is a recreational playground for everyone, with amusement rides and theme park–style attractions for families with children, and nice white-sand beaches for sun worshippers.

DISTANCE: 4km (2.5 miles)
TIME: A full day, or overnight
START: Resorts World Sentosa
END: Wings of TIme
POINTS TO NOTE: The fastest way to the island is to take the Sentosa Express light rail (daily 7am–midnight) from VivoCity mall Lobby L, Level 3 on the mainland. It takes less than 5 minutes to reach Imbiah Station. To get to VivoCity, take the MRT to HarbourFront station. You can also get to Sentosa by taxi or cable car (tel: 6377 9688; www.faber peaksingapore.com; daily 8.45am–10pm, last boarding 9.30pm). On the island, you can walk, or take the light rail or the free bus services and beach trams. Alternatively, get to the island on foot via the Sentosa Boardwalk. Stroll from VivoCity's waterfront promenade to Sentosa along a covered travellator (daily 7am–midnight).

Sentosa (www.sentosa.com.sg), located to the south of the main island, was once known as Pulau Blakang Mati ('island at the back of death' in Malay) because of the frequent outbreaks of fatal disease. Before it was turned into a leisure playground and renamed Sentosa, which means 'isle of peace and tranquility' in Malay, it was at different times a refuge for pirates, a military garrison, and a detention centre for citizens arrested under the Internal Security Act.

Today, Sentosa is filled with activities and attractions. It has something for everyone, from historical sights to laid-back beaches to child-centric attractions. It would be too exhausting to see all the attractions in a single day. This itinerary covers the highlights. If you are inspired to see more, stay overnight at one of the hotels or resorts (see page 109).

Resorts World Sentosa
After an extensive redevelopment, Sentosa today is a must-visit spot, especially for families. The sprawling 'integrated resort' **Resorts World Sentosa ❶** (www.rwsentosa.com) boasts a casino, mid-range and upscale hotels and restaurants as well as a slew of high-end

Sentosa has an idyllic tropical setting

boutiques. The biggest draw here is the Universal Studios theme park, the only one in Southeast Asia.

The nearest train stop is Waterfront Station. Hop off and have breakfast at **Toast Box**, see ❶. Then head to **Universal Studios Singapore** (Mon–Sun 10am–7pm, Sat 10am–8pm, operating hours subject to change). You can spend an entire day exploring the seven zones and 24 attractions, of which 18 are exclusively designed for Singapore. Online pre-booking is usually necessary, especially during the busy school holidays.

Universal Studios

Other attractions include a Marine Life Park, touted as the world's largest oceanarium. You can easily spend an entire day here. Within the park is the S.E.A. Aquarium (daily 10am–7pm), which has more than 800 species of marine animals and over 200 sharks. At the Adventure Cove Waterpark (daily 10am–6pm), you can snorkel with 20,000 tropical fish or float down Adventure River, passing through 14 themed zones. Over at the Maritime Experiential Museum, experience an interactive voyage along the ancient Maritime Silk Route and the 360-degree multi-sensor Typhoon Theatre.

IMBIAH LOOKOUT

To enjoy great views of the Singapore harbour and the surrounding islands, there are two options close to Imbiah Station, though it's only worth ascending on clear days. One is the 110m (360-ft) **Tiger Sky Tower ❷** (www.skytower.com. sg; daily 9am–9pm), whose lift whisks you up for a view from 131m (430-ft) above sea level. The other is the 37m (120-ft) **Merlion ❸** (daily 10am–8pm; charge), which is also the focus of a show with smoke and laser lights at night. Head across Merlion Plaza to the escalators to visit the recently-opened **Madame Tussauds Singapore**.

Thrill rides
Kids and thrill-seekers will like the **Skyline Luge Sentosa ❹** (daily 10am–9.30pm; charge). After buying your ticket

at the booth near Beach Station, ascend a slope by a four-seater chairlift and whizz down a 650-m/yd paved track in a luge, which is a cross between a go-kart and a toboggan.

Near the top of the Skyride is **Sentosa 4D Adventureland ❺** (www.4dadventure land.com.sg; daily 10am–9pm, last show at 8.45pm), with an engaging 4D movie experience. More gripping action is found at the high-tech **Sentosa Cine-Blast ❻** (daily 10am–9pm), located behind 4D Magix.

Butterfly Park & Insect Kingdom
For something more subdued, stroll through the lush grounds of the **Butterfly Park & Insect Kingdom ❼** (www.jungle. com.sg; daily 9.30am–7pm), located next to Sentosa 4D Adventureland. As many as 1,500 butterflies from more than 50 species, including some endangered ones, flutter around in this conservatory. It is also home to over 3,000 species of insects.

Images of Singapore
The best attraction in the Imbiah cluster is **Images of Singapore ❽** (daily 9am–7pm). Housed in a former military hospital, this museum has waxwork exhibits that recount Singapore's social history.

Nature Walk
Nature lovers can explore the 1.5km (1-mile)-long **Nature Walk ❾**, which starts from the Cable Car Arrival Plaza. Wander through a secondary rainforest

Sentosa has some fine beaches

and look out for vegetation such as the insectivorous pitcher plants and huge Tembusu trees.

BEACHES

Although the views are somewhat marred by container ships in the distance, Sentosa's beaches are probably Singapore's finest stretches of sand, running some 3km (2 miles) along the southern shore of the resort island and interspersed with scenic lagoons and coconut groves.

Siloso Beach
Siloso Beach ❿ is a hotspot for watersports and beach volleyball. From here you can head out to sea on rental windsurfers, canoes and pedal boats, join bare-chested young men and bikini-clad ladies for a game of volleyball, or chill out at **Trapizza**, see ❷, a nice spot for a cool beer and lunch. If you want to fly like a circus performer, head to Siloso Beach's **Flying Trapeze** (Mon–Fri 2.30–6.30pm, Sat, Sun 2.30–7pm). An instructor will be at hand to supervise your 'stunt'.

Adventure-seekers can free-fall through the air at **iFly Singapore** (www. iflysingapore.com; Mon, Tue, Thu–Sun 9am–10pm, Wed 10.30am–10pm), the world's largest themed wind tunnel for indoor skydiving. This attraction is located beside the Beach Station. About five minutes' walk from this station is **Wavehouse Sentosa** (www.wavehouse sentosa.com; daily 10.30am–10.30pm; charge). There, surfers, both novices and experts, can enjoy riding 10-foot man-made waves. After hanging up your wetsuit, you can sip cocktails, have a bite and listen to live music.

Palawan Beach
Over at **Palawan Beach** ⓫, you can climb onto the **suspension bridge**, which links the main island to a tiny islet billed as the southernmost point of continental Asia. On the islet are two towers, clad in wood and bamboo, that afford a view of the sea. Near the beach is the Palawan Amphitheatre, the venue of **Animal & Bird Encounters** ⓬, where the audience can snuggle up to snakes, primates and birds during performances.

In the next five years, Sentosa's planned makeover will dedicate the Palawan Beach area increasingly to family activities.

Tanjong Beach
On the eastern side of Sentosa is **Tanjong Beach** ⓭, a more peaceful and secluded spot removed from the madding crowd, great for relaxing with a book and cool drink.

DOLPHIN LAGOON

Along Palawan Beach also sits the **Dolphin Lagoon** ⓮ (daily 10.30am–6pm; charge includes entry to the Underwater World), where rare and intelligent pink dolphins, also known as Indo-Pacific Humpbacked Dolphins, present their

Fort Siloso

tail-flapping antics in 'Meet the Dolphin and Fur Seals' shows (11am, 2, 4 and 5.45pm). If you book ahead (tel: 6275 0030; extra charge), you can have a closer encounter, including a swim in the lagoon with the dolphins.

UNDERWATER WORLD

Your ticket to the Dolphin Lagoon also admits you into the **Underwater World** ⑮ (www.underwaterworld.com.sg; daily 10am–7pm), a sanctuary for more than 2,500 sea creatures, located on the western end of the island. As you journey through the 'ocean', or rather, an 83m/yd-long acrylic tunnel, on a travelator, you are surrounded by marine life of every imaginable kind, from stingrays and reef sharks to turtles and jellyfish.

Don't miss the Living Fossils exhibit, where about 20 fish, including the massive arapaima, which can grow up to 3m (10ft), and the pacu, a tamer cousin of the piranha, have been tagged with microchips. When a tagged fish swims past a sensor, information such as its species and origin is displayed on an LCD touchscreen. After your tour, try fish reflexology at the Underwater World.

FORT SILOSO

Near the Underwater World is another of Sentosa's history displays and one of its must-sees, **Fort Siloso** ⑯ (daily 10am–6pm). During World War II, the British pointed all their guns and cannons at this fort out to sea. This proved futile as the Japanese unexpectedly invaded overland from the north via the Malayan peninsula.

The armoury and cannons are still on display. The Surrender Chambers here bring to life Singapore's formal surrender to the Japanese in 1942 through a mix of gripping real audio-visual footage, artefacts and realistic wax figurines.

SENTOSA COVE AND QUAYSIDE ISLE

At one edge of the island is **Sentosa Cove** ⑰, a posh residential area with multi-million dollar homes, and Quayside Isle, a dining enclave facing a marina filled with bobbing yachts. Well-heeled locals and expats frequent the many restaurants at the weekend. Right at the end of Quayside Isle is W Singapore, which attracts the trendy set to its host of lively parties and events.

EVENING ENTERTAINMENT

End the day at **Wings of Time** ⑱ (Siloso Beach; www.wingsoftime.com.sg; daily 7.40pm and 8.40pm), a multi-sensorial night show set in the open sea. Little ones will enjoy the contemporary storyline showcasing multimedia effects including 3D projection mapping, state-of-the-art-lasers, robotic water fountains, giant water jets and pyrotechnics.

Sentosa has no lack of dinner

The Wings of Time show

Dolphin Show at Underwater World

options, with a number of restaurants that are ranked among the best in Singapore. Recommended are **The Cliff**, see ❸, **Forest**, see ❹, **Skirt**, see ❺ and **Saint Pierre**, see ❻.

Sentosa's chill out spots are concentrated on the beaches. Over at Tanjong Beach, party-goers can sip cocktails and enjoy the sunset at Tanjong Beach Club (www.tanjongbeachclub.com).

Food and drink

❶ TOAST BOX
26 Sentosa Gateway, Resorts World #B1-203/204; tel 6686 3764; daily 24 hours; $
Have a local breakfast of kaya toast, soft boiled eggs and freshly brewed coffee. For something more substantial, slurp up spicy noodles such as *laksa* and *mee siam*.

❷ TRAPIZZA
Siloso Beach; tel: 6376 2662; www.shangri-la.com; daily 11.30am–9.30pm; $$$
Trapizza is an outdoor Italian-style restaurant run by Rasa Sentosa Resort. Its menu includes wood-fired pizzas, pastas and other casual fare. There is also a children's set menu.

❸ THE CLIFF
The Singapore Resort & Spa Sentosa, 2 Bukit Manis Road; tel: 6371 1425; www.singaporeresortsentosa.com; daily 6.30pm–midnight; $$$$
Amid The Cliff's romantic setting by the sea, dine on the finest seafood as well as contemporary creations. There is also a good selection of French oysters.

❹ FOREST
8 Sentosa Gateway, Resorts World Sentosa,
Level 1, Equarius Hotel; tel: 6577 6688; Mon–Sat noon–2.30pm, Sun noon–3pm, Mon–Sun 6–10.30pm; $$$$
Modern Chinese restaurant by celebrity chef Sam Leong with a theatre kitchen where you can watch your meals being whipped up.

❺ SAINT PIERRE
31 Ocean Way, 01-15 Quayside Isle; tel: 6438 0887; www.saintpierre.com.sg; Tue–Fri 5.30pm–midnight, Sat 11.30–3pm, 5.30pm–midnight, Sun 11.30am–10.30pm; $$$$
After relocating from the city to Sentosa Cove, this well-established modern French restaurant owned by celebrity chef Emmanuel Stroobant continues to wow diners with his sophisticated seasonal menu. Signatures include Stroobant's foie gras creations and oven-baked black cod with white miso.

❻ SKIRT
21 Ocean Way; W Singapore – Sentosa Cove; tel: 6808 7278; www.wsingaporesentosacove.com; daily 6pm–midnight; $$$$
A vibrant dining experience awaits meat lovers at Skirt. Beef is aged in glass cabinets and chefs fire up all cuts of meats in the open kitchen right in the centre of the restaurant.

The Imperial Cheng Ho cruise

SOUTHERN ISLANDS

Around Sentosa is a cluster of islets known as the Southern Islands, comprising Kusu, a place of rest and worship; St John's, a holiday spot with an easygoing air; and Sisters' Islands and Pulau Hantu, both popular diving areas.

DISTANCE: 13km (8 miles)
round trip
TIME: Half a day
START/END: Marina South Pier
POINTS TO NOTE: To get to the Marina South Pier, take bus no. 402 from the Marina Bay MRT station.

You could do this route on your own. A ferry service, which first stops at St John's Island followed by Kusu Island, is run by **Singapore Island Cruises** (www.islandcruise.com.sg). To get to Sisters' Islands or Pulau Hantu, charter a boat.

A more leisurely way to enjoy views of Singapore's harbour and the soaring cityscape from the sea is the 2.5-hour Imperial Cheng Ho cruise on a replica Chinese junk, operated by **Watertours Pte Ltd** (www.watertours.com.sg). The cruise departs from the Marina South Pier and makes a half-hour stop at Kusu Island, passing St John's and other scenic islands along the way.

Tua Pek Kong temple on Kusu Island

KUSU ISLAND

Kusu ❶, which means 'Tortoise Island' in the Chinese Hokkien dialect, is located about 6km (3.5 miles) south of the Singapore island. Legend has it that two shipwrecked sailors, Malay and Chinese, were saved by a tortoise that transformed itself into an island. Each man gave thanks and built a place of worship according to his own belief.

About 130,000 worshippers throng Kusu during the ninth lunar month of the calendar, usually between September and November. During other times of the year, the island is quieter. The island can be covered on foot in less than an hour.

Day-trippers can enjoy a dip in the two lagoons, which are also good spots for picnicking. There are many shady trees and picnic tables as well as public toilets and showers. It is best to pack your own food and drinks for a picnic.

Overnight stays are not allowed on Kusu Island, so don't miss the last ferry.

Chinese Temple

The Taoist **Tua Pek Kong Temple** was actually built by a well-to-do merchant in 1923. It has classical Chinese green-tiled roofs and red walls and is reached via a series of pavilion-studded bridges set over a picturesque lagoon. Besides the Tua Pek Kong, the God of Prosperity, Guan Yin, the Goddess of Mercy, is also enshrined here. Also check out the **Tortoise Sanctuary**, filled with hundreds of tortoises.

Muslim shrines

Climb 152 steps to the summit of the hill. Standing here are three Muslim *keramat* (shrines), built to pay tribute to a devout man, Syed Abdul Rahman, his mother and sister, who lived in the 19th century. These are popular with childless couples who come to pray for fertility.

ST JOHN'S ISLAND

Situated approximately 6.5km (4 miles) south of Singapore, the 39-hectare (96-acre) **St John's Island ❷** is a peaceful getaway with sandy beaches, lagoons, holiday bungalows and plenty of flora and fauna. This was where Raffles' ship anchored before he met the Malay chief on Singapore island in 1819. St John's served as a quarantine centre for immigrants until the 1950s before it was used as a holding centre for political detainees.

PULAU HANTU AND SISTERS' ISLANDS

Pulau Hantu ❸ (Ghost Island), to the northwest of Sentosa, was named so because it was said to be haunted by the spirits of two ancient warriors who fought to their deaths here. Enveloped by coral reefs, it is regarded as one of Singapore's best diving spots.

Singapore's richest coral reefs line the coasts of the two isles known as **Sisters' Islands ❹**, to the west of St John's Island. The currents can get strong here so be cautious when swimming.

An Indian peacock at Jurong BirdPark

WESTERN SINGAPORE

This part of the island has several attractions worth seeing, especially if you have kids in tow. The Jurong BirdPark and the Science Centre appeal to inquisitive minds, while the Chinese Garden offers quiet respite.

DISTANCE: Varies
TIME: A full day
START: Jurong BirdPark
END: Singapore Science Centre
POINTS TO NOTE: These attractions are not located near each other. To get to the bird park, take the MRT to Boon Lay station and transfer to bus no. 194 or 251. A daily bus service (charge) goes from VivoCity and bus stops near some downtown hotels. To go on to the Science Centre, take a taxi or the MRT to Jurong East station and transfer to bus no. 335.

Western Singapore, although designated as the country's industrial zone, has sprawling green spaces and a few family-friendly theme parks.

JURONG BIRDPARK

The 20-hectare (49-acre) **Jurong BirdPark ❶** (2 Jurong Hill; www.birdpark.com.sg; daily 8.30am–6pm) is home to some 5,000 birds across 400 different species. The landscaped grounds make for a pleasant walk. You can also hop onto the air-conditioned, elevated **Panorail** (separate charge) for more dramatic views.

Check the information board for the show times and plan your route accordingly. Highly entertaining shows include Kings of the Skies (daily 10am and 4pm) starring eagles, vultures and owls, and the High Flyers Show (daily 11am and 3pm) featuring parrots, hornbills and flamingos.

Jurong Falls

A parrot at a Jurong BirdPark show

As you walk in from the entrance, you will see the **Penguin Coast** which houses six species of penguins including the regal King Penguin and the tiny Fairy Penguin. Other attractions include the **Parrot Paradise** with the park's most colourful and friendly residents and the **Pelican Cove**, where visitors can view underwater feeding of pelicans.

The **Southeast Asian Birds Aviary** is a lush walk-through rainforest with a simulated thunderstorm at noon. Look out for the feeding areas, where fruit is placed. Another outstanding attraction is the **Lory Loft**, a walk-in aviary hosting some 1,000 free-flying lories. From the boardwalk and the suspension bridge 12m (40ft) above ground, you take in 360-degree views of the simulated Australian Outback.

Around the walk-in **Waterfall Aviary**, with the thunderous man-made **Jurong Falls**, birds originating from Africa and South America fly free.

Kiosks around the park offer snacks and light meals. Otherwise, have a bite at **Bongo Burgers**, see ❶.

CHINESE GARDEN

A short taxi ride from the bird park is the **Jurong Lake**, the setting for the **Chinese Garden** ❷ (1 Chinese Garden Road; daily 6am–11pm; free). Its theme gardens, fashioned in the style of the Summer Palace in Beijing, are a harmonious blend of natural and man-made elements such as rocks, ponds, streams, bridges and footpaths. The lovely twin pagodas have nice views of the lake.

SCIENCE CENTRE

Move on to the **Science Centre** ❸ (15 Science Centre Road; www.science.edu.sg; daily 10am–6pm), which has 1,000 science exhibits in its 14 galleries.

Highlights include the **Genome Exhibit**, where DNA structures are explored through 3D exhibits. Optical illusions are found in the **Mind's Eye Gallery**, and children will find the sculptures and water features in the **Kinetic Garden** especially engaging. The adjacent **Omni-Theatre** screens IMAX movies (daily noon–7pm).

If you're hungry, walk from Jurong East MRT to JEM mall, which has many food outlets such as **Din Tai Fung**, see ❷.

Food and drink

❶ BONGO BURGERS
Jurong BirdPark; tel: 6265 0022; Mon–Fri 10am–6pm, Sat–Sun 8.30am–6.30pm; $$
Burgers in generous American-sized servings, plus a selection of other dishes like jumbo hot dogs and fish and chips.

❷ DIN TAI FUNG
50 Jurong Gateway Road, 02-07 JEM; tel: 6694 1161; www.dintaifung.com.sg; Mon–Fri 11am–10pm Sat–Sun 10am–10pm; $$
This popular restaurant offers dumplings, steamed buns, and noodle dishes.

Singapore city centre from Mount Faber

SOUTHERN SINGAPORE

The summit of Mount Faber is an ideal spot to take in panoramic views of Singapore's harbour. After the sun has set, swing by VivoCity, the city's largest mall, for a shopping spree or a meal at one of its many eateries.

DISTANCE: 1.5km (1 mile)
TIME: Half a day
START: Mount Faber
END: VivoCity
POINTS TO NOTE: Start this tour in the late afternoon. To ascend Mount Faber, take a taxi or the cable car.

Exit the HarbourFront MRT station from Exit D to Marang Road. This road leads to the **Marang Trail**, with stairs and shaded footpaths weaving through a secondary forest. The walk takes 15 to 20 minutes. The Marang Trail connects to Faber Walk, leading to the cable car station and **Faber Peak Singapore** (www.faberpeaksingapore.com; daily 8.30am–11pm) on the

Southern Singapore is most well known for the Port of Singapore and as the gateway to Sentosa (see page 76).

MOUNT FABER

Mount Faber ❶ is a 110m (360-ft) -high hill blanketed by one of the oldest rainforests in Singapore. Formerly called Telok Blangah Hill, it was renamed after Captain C.E. Faber of the Madras Engineers, who built the road to the summit.

In VivoCity

summit. From here, enjoy vistas of the harbour and the city, especially delightful at sunset. Have a pre-dinner drink and bites at **Moonstone**, a yakitori-sake bar. When you have had your fill of the views, retrace your steps down the hill (the Marang Trail is deliberately unlit after dark to minimise disturbance to nocturnal life, so bring a torch if you choose to take this trail). Otherwise, call for a taxi. For something a little more dramatic, opt for a cable-car ride down to HarbourFront. For a unique experience, book the Sky Dining experience where you can take in the views of the skyline while you dine in a cable car drifting between Mount Faber and Sentosa 70m (230ft) above the sea (reservations: tel: 6377 9688; www.faber peaksingapore.com).

VIVOCITY

Japanese architect Toyo Ito created a fluid facade that evokes sea waves for **VivoCity** ❷ (1 Harbourfront Walk; tel: 6377 6860; www.vivocity.com.sg; daily 10am–10pm). It has hundreds of stores and restaurants; in fact this mall is so huge you will need more than half a day to cover it thoroughly. Browse at leisure or head to one of its many food and beverage outlets such as **The Queen and Mangosteen**, see ❶, or **Signatures by Tung Lok**, see ❷.

Haw Par Villa

Also known as Tiger Balm Gardens, Haw Par Villa (meaning 'villa of the tiger and the leopard') was named after its owners, the brothers behind the famous Tiger Balm ointment. Built in 1937, the park features statues that illustrate Chinese mythological stories and notorious crimes. When Boon Par died in 1945, Boon Haw turned it into a public park. With its stagnant ponds and faded statues, the park has seen better days, but it is a quirky sight whose gaudiness has to be seen to be believed. To get there (262 Pasir Panjang Road; daily 9am–7pm; free), take bus no. 188 from the HarbourFront Bus Interchange or bus no. 200 from the Buona Vista MRT station.

Food and drink

❶ THE QUEEN AND MANGOSTEEN
#01-106-107 VivoCity 1, Harbourfront Walk; tel: 6376 9380; Sun–Thu 11am–midnight Fri–Sat 1am; $$
This British gourmet pub overlooks the waterfront and Sentosa Island. The kitchen dishes out pub grub.

❷ SIGNATURES BY TUNG LOK
01-57 VivoCity; tel: 6376 9555; www.tunglok.com; Mon–Sat 11.30am–3pm and 6–10.30pm, Sun 11am–3.30pm and 6–10.30pm; $$$
Cantonese, Shanghainese and Sichuan dishes woven with creativity are served in a chic decor surrounded by nice harbour views.

Ornate terrace houses on Koon Seng Road

KATONG AND THE EAST COAST

Known for laid-back, beachside living, Katong in eastern Singapore is also a veritable living museum of Straits Chinese culture, with decades-old Peranakan eateries and floridly decorated conservation terrace houses.

DISTANCE: 2km (1.25 miles), more if you want to explore the East Coast Park

TIME: A half/full day

START: Kuan Im Tng Temple

END: East Coast Park

POINTS TO NOTE: To get to the start of this route, ake a short taxi ride from the Paya Lebar MRT station to Tembeling Road.

Katong is roughly bounded by Tanjong Katong Road, Mountbatten and East Coast roads, Changi Road and Telok Kurau Road. In the early 19th century, Katong was situated just by the sea. Portuguese and Chinese settlers planted cotton, coconut and gambier in the area, whose name was derived from a species of sea turtle that was once found in Singapore. After World War I, it became home to well-heeled Chinese, Peranakans and Eurasians.

Due to land shortage in the 1970s, this area was reclaimed, all the way to the East Coast Parkway.

JOO CHIAT

The first stop of the walk is **Kuan Im Tng Temple ❶** at no. 62 on Tembeling Road, which is parallel to Joo Chiat Road. This ornate temple, with dancing dragons adorning its roofs and pillars, was built in 1921. It is dedicated to Buddhism, Taoism and Confucianism, with the Jade Emperor, the Goddess of Mercy (Guan Yin), the God of War (Guan Di), and several other deities enshrined in the prayer hall.

Note its courtyard wall of Chinese paintings, illustrating classic stories of filial piety.

KOON SENG ROAD

Exit the temple and turn right on Tembeling Road. When you come to **Koon Seng Road ❷**, turn right. The row of prewar conservation terrace houses is a perfect showcase of the flamboyant Peranakan architectural style. Before World War II, many wealthy Peranakans built lavish homes that displayed a unique fusion of Chinese, Malay

Sri Senpaga Vinayagar Temple

and European design elements. Typically these houses are underscored by plasterwork with flora and fauna motifs and intricate tiles, and feature a pair of carved wooden *pintu pagar* ('fence doors').

Continue to Joo Chiat Road, where you can hire a taxi to get to the next stop, Ceylon Road. If you choose to go on foot, note that it will be a lengthy walk with not much, except bungalows and apartment blocks, to see.

ST HILDA'S CHURCH

At the junction of Ceylon and Fowlie roads stands the 1934 **St Hilda's Anglican Church 3** (41 Ceylon Road; http://sthildas.org.sg; daily 9am–

6pm). Fashioned after an English parish church, the building is topped by a Victorian-style conical tower and features beautiful stained glass.

SENPAGA TEMPLE

A 5-minute walk from St Hilda's Anglican Church is one of Singapore's oldest Hindu shrines, the **Sri Senpaga Vinayagar Temple 4** (19 Ceylon Road; www.senpaga.org.sg; daily 5.30am–12.30pm and 5.30–11pm). It dates back to the 1850s, when a statue of Lord Vinayagar, the Elephant God, was unearthed by the side of a pond. A Ceylonese (Sri Lankan) Tamil built the first temple structure, which was a simple shelter with a thatched *attap* (nipa) roof, positioned under a *senpaga* (Chempaka) tree. When the area was bombed during World War II, the main shrine remained intact.

Today the temple, rebuilt in 1989, is an important place of worship for the Hindu community living in the eastern part of Singapore island. It is especially noted for its 20m (65ft) -high *gopuram* (tower), above its entrance, which bears no less than 159 sculptures of Hindu gods and deities.

EAST COAST ROAD

After your temple visit, continue on Ceylon Road to **East Coast Road**. Stop by **Casa Bom Vento 1** for a meal of Peranakan and Eurasian fare.

Katong Antique House

Peranakan culture

Back on East Coast Road, drop by **Kim Choo** (111 East Coast Road; www.kim choo.com; daily 8am–9pm), a business started by Madam Lee Kim Choo in the late 1940s. She first learned her grandmother's secret recipe of making glutinous rice dumplings at the age of 12, and went on to support her four children by selling these dumplings. She has since handed over her thriving business to them. Upstairs is a gallery; Kim Choo's grandson, Raymond Wong, will gladly show you his collection of Peranakan artefacts, such as quality porcelain from Jiangxi, China, vintage batiks and intricate beaded slippers. One of the best souvenirs you can take away from here is a *sarong kebaya* (Nonya blouse and sarong skirt) with delicate embroidery. Demonstrations of dumpling-making are also offered here.

Just next door is **Rumah Bebe** ➎ (no. 113; www.rumahbebe.com; Tue–Sun 9.30am–6.30pm), a treasure trove of all things Peranakan, from furnishings and traditional apparel to jewellery and porcelain, housed in. a 1928 shophouse. It is owned by former school teacher and renowned beadwork specialist Bebe Seet. Look out for the lovely bridal chamber on level two and intricate *kasut manik manik*, dainty slippers of fine beadwork. Bebe also conducts bi-weekly beading classes to keep the craft, which is on the brink of vanishing, alive.

Another stop for Peranakan treats is **Glory Catering**, see ➋.

Church of the Holy Family

East Coast Road is a long road. You can end your Katong tour after your meal, or explore a couple of other places along the stretch.

Generations of Peranakan and Eurasian Roman Catholics living in the east have worshipped at the **Church of the Holy Family** ➏ (6 Chapel Road; www.holyfamily.org.sg; daily 6am–7.30pm). In 1923, a chapel was built on this site and subsequently torn down to make way for this church, which was completed in 1932.

Katong Antique House

Further down from the church is the **Katong Antique House** ➐ (208 East Coast Road, tel: 6345 8544; open by appointment only), an iconic shop owned by Peter Wee. He is a fourth-generation Baba who began his business of buying, restoring and selling Peranakan furniture, porcelain and other cultural products in 1971. The shop is a treasure trove of traditional crockery, jewellery, beaded slippers, costumes and furniture. A small gallery sits on the upper level of the shophouse. Peter has in-depth knowledge of his heritage, so make an appointment if you want to hear fascinating stories of yore.

A few doors down from the antique shop is **328 Katong Laksa**, see ➌, where you can enjoy the area's signa-

Cycling in East Coast Park

ture noodle dish. For something lighter, drop by **Chin Mee Chin**, see ❹.

EAST COAST PARK

Take a 5-minute taxi ride from East Coast Road to the **East Coast Park ❺** further south. The beach park, stretching about 20km (12 miles) between the Changi Airport and Marina Bay, is a popular playground and dining destination.

The 7.5km (4.5-mile) reclaimed beach is just narrow slopes of not-so-fine sand, and the waters are rather murky and not recommended for swimming.

Locals, however, don't complain, as the balmy environment, with views of ships anchored in the Strait of Singapore, is refreshing after a week of toiling in air-conditioned offices. At the weekends the park teems with picnicking families, joggers, bladers and cyclists. If you want to catch a glimpse of Singaporeans at play, the park is a good place.

Like elsewhere in Singapore, the East Coast Park offers plenty to eat. The restaurants at the **East Coast Seafood Centre**, famed for Singapore-style seafood dishes like chilli and pepper crabs, are persistently booked out.

Food and drink

❶ CASA BOM VENTO

477 Joo Chiat Road; tel: 6440 0196; daily 11.30am–3pm and 5.30–9.30pm; $$
This homey family run restaurant serves Eurasian and Peranakan dishes. The unique Eurasian cuisine is an amalgamation of Portuguese and local flavours. Most dishes served are spicy yet heartwarming.

❷ GLORY CATERING

139 East Coast Road; tel: 6344 1749; www.glorycatering.com.sg; Tue–Sun 8.30am–8.30pm; $–$$
Another old-time favourite, well loved for its *nasi padang* (rice with Indonesian-style dishes) and Peranakan sweet treats like pineapple tarts and coconut-milk-infused cookies and cakes.

❸ 328 KATONG LAKSA

216/218 East Coast Road; daily 10am–9pm; http://328katonglaksa.com.sg; $
Many eateries in this area claim that they serve the best laksa (thick rice noodles in a rich, spicy coconut-milk-based gravy). 328 Katong Laksa is largely acknowledged as one of the best.

❹ CHIN MEE CHIN

204 East Coast Road; tel: 6345 0419; Tue–Sun 8.30am–5pm; $
This bakery and coffee shop hasn't changed much since it opened more than six decades ago. Loyal customers, spanning generations, have been coming here for coffee served in traditional porcelain cups, alongside soft-boiled eggs and *kaya* (coconut jam) toast. Traditional jam rolls, buns and cakes are popular for afternoon tea.

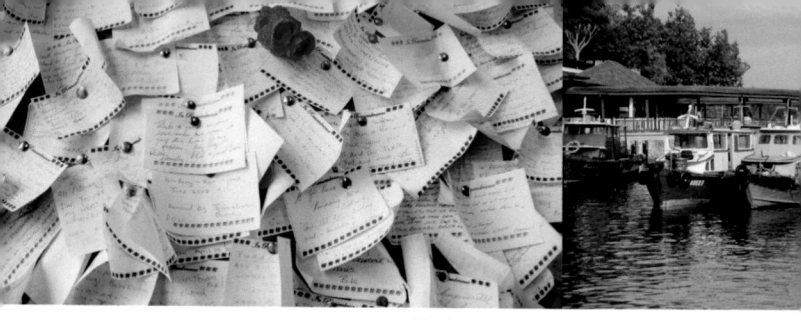

The Changi Museum

CHANGI

Peaceful Changi provides a welcome contrast to the frenzied city. Its star attraction is the poignant Changi Chapel and Museum, while laid-back Changi Village appeals with its restful and breezy atmosphere.

DISTANCE: 5.5km (3.5 miles)
TIME: Half a day
START: Changi Chapel and Museum
END: Changi Beach Park
POINTS TO NOTE: Take a taxi to the Changi Museum or hop on bus no. 2 from the Tanah Merah MRT station. The bus stops opposite the museum. Take bus no. 2 from the same bus stop to Changi Village. To get to Pulau Ubin, walk to Changi Point Ferry Terminal (tel: 6542 7944), a few minutes from Changi Village Hawker Centre, and take a 10-minute bumboat ride (daily 6am–8pm; charge; boats leave when there are 12 passengers).

Changi is most well known as the location of Singapore's airport, but it also contains a few gems.

CHANGI CHAPEL AND MUSEUM

During the Japanese Occupation from 1942 to 1945, the Japanese army turned British-built barracks in Changi into a prisoner-of-war (POW) camp. It was a notorious hellhole where thousands of military and civilian prisoners were interned and endured appalling conditions.

Built in 1988, the **Changi Chapel and Museum** ❶ (1000 Upper Changi Road North; www.changimuseum.sg; daily 9.30am–5pm; free) is dedicated to the POWs who were interned at Changi camp.

The **museum** provides moving insights into the POWs' lives in the Changi internment camp, which housed as many as 3,000 prisoners at one time. Among the exhibits are poignant letters, photographs, and personal effects donated by former POWs and their families, which portray the POWs' suffering and hope during those dark years. Especially notable are the sketches and paintings by William Haxworth and photographs by George Aspinall.

Changi Murals

The museum also features a replica of the Changi Murals. The Japanese military allowed a ward in the internment camp to be used as a chapel. Bombardier Stanley Warren, of the 15th Field Regiment, decorated the chapel

Boats at Changi Point jetty　　　　　　　　　*The Changi Chapel*

with life-sized murals that depicted scenes from the life of Christ. These original murals, known as the **Changi Murals**, are now in the grounds of an operational military camp – Block 151 of Changi Airbase – and are open for public viewing only during four window periods in February, August, September and November. Visitors who wish to view them must apply at least two weeks ahead to the public relations department of the Ministry of Defence (24-hour hotline at 9228 6190). For many years after the war, the murals lay hidden and forgotten as the ward was used as a storage room, and were only discovered during renovations in 1958.

Changi Chapel

The **Changi Chapel** is a replica of one of many similar places of worship erected by POWs while incarcerated in Changi camp. The original was dismantled after World War II and reassembled in Australia. This replica was built in 1988 in

Pulau Ubin

Located off Singapore's northeastern tip, Pulau Ubin (Granite Island) measures just 8km (5 miles) across and 1.5km (1 mile) wide. It is home to Singapore's last *kampung* (village), with about 100 villagers who still depend on well water and on diesel generators for electricity. Stop by the National Parks Board (NParks) information kiosk (daily 8.30am–5pm) to pick up a map and leaflets with details on the island's flora and fauna. In Ubin town there are bicycle rental shops, eateries and provision shops. It is best to see the island on a bike; three cycling trails go past fruit and rubber plantations, mangrove swamps and quarry pits.

Sunset at Changi Bay

response to requests by former POWs and their families.

The chapel sits in a garden with hibiscus and frangipani plants. You are welcome to leave a flower on the altar or a note on a board to the left of the altar in remembrance of the POWs.

CHANGI VILLAGE

When you are done at the museum and chapel, hop on a 10–15 minute bus or taxi ride to **Changi Village ❷**. Along the way you can see Changi Prison and various military sites behind barbed wire fencing. When you reach Changi Village, head to the **hawker centre ❶**, see located next to the bus terminus, for lunch.

Take time to wander around the sleepy village, a slice of charming old Singa-

pore. Seafood restaurants and pubs also line Netheravon Road, while the **Village Hotel Changi** (tel: 6379 7111; www.stay fareast.com) offers the only hotel accommodation in the area.

Changi Village is also home to a variety of splendid old trees. The magnificent *Shorea Gibbosa* tree, which has a cauliflower-like crown, at the junction of Netheravon and Turnhouse roads, is said to be one of the last two left in Singapore.

A short walk from the hawker centre is the **Changi Point Ferry Terminal**, where you depart on a bumboat ride to **Pulau Ubin**.

CHANGI BEACH PARK

Take the footbridge to the 3km (2-mile)-long **Changi Beach Park ❸**. Changi Beach is a craggy stretch, so don't expect soft white sand under your feet. Higher tides can conceal sharp rocks; be careful if you are wading in the water.

Still, the beach is popular with locals who come to picnic, fish at the pier, enjoy the sea breeze and watch planes land and take off from the Changi Airport.

Changi Massacre Site

Further east on Changi Beach is the **Changi Massacre Site ❹**, marked by a storyboard. This was where the sand was reported to have turned red with blood on 20 February 1942. Sixty-six Chinese men thought to be anti-Japanese sympathisers were lined up along the water's edge and killed by a Japanese firing squad.

Food and drink

❶ CHANGI VILLAGE HAWKER CENTRE

01-08 Changi Village Market and Food Centre, 2 Changi Village Road; daily early morning till late; $–$$

Recommended are Wing Kee (01-04) for its *hor fun* (flat rice noodles) with beef or seafood, and International (01-57) for its *nasi lemak*. But it is Charlie's Corner (01-08; tel: 6542 0867) that has been the favourite since the late 1970s. Offering a huge selection of beer and old-school pub grub, it is packed at the weekend. The stall is closed on Monday, when Charlie is out fishing.

Boardwalk through the rainforest

BUKIT TIMAH NATURE RESERVE

A Sanctuary containing one of Singapore's two virgin rainforests and a rich biodiversity, this reserve is easily accessed from the city centre. Hike up to the hilltop for good views and spot tropical flora and fauna along the way.

DISTANCE: 1km (0.6 mile)

TIME: 2–3 hours

START/END: Bukit Timah Nature Reserve Visitor Centre

POINTS TO NOTE: This is best as a morning excursion. Allow 30 minutes to get there from the city centre. From the Newton MRT station, bus no. 67, 170 or 171 takes you to Upper Bukit Timah Road. Alight at Bukit Timah Shopping Centre, cross Jalan Anak Bukit, walk up Hindhede Road and then to the end of Hindhede Drive. Going by taxi is by far the easiest way. Have the driver drop you off at the car park. (Note: The reserve will be limited to the public for two years from September 2014 as the National Parks Board carries out repair and restoration works; visit: www.nparks.gov.sg.)

The **Bukit Timah Nature Reserve** (177 Hindhede Drive; tel: 6468 5736; www. nparks.gov.sg; daily 6am–7pm; free) is located almost in the geographic centre of Singapore, 12km (7.5 miles) from the city. It contains Singapore's highest hill, the **Bukit Timah Hill**, at 164m (538ft) above sea level and offers 164 hectares (405 acres) of ecologically important lowland rainforest.

BACKGROUND

Most of Singapore's forest was heavily logged until the mid-19th century. In 1884, in response to research commissioned by the Straits Settlements government on climatic changes arising from deforestation, the Bukit Timah Nature

Enjoying the trails

Reserve was established. For more than a century, the forest was a botanical collecting ground.

The reserve has suffered significant changes in its biodiversity levels due to the poaching of animals and logging in the early 20th century and more recent urban encroachments. Large mammals like tigers and deer no longer roam the forest and ecologically rare birds like hornbills and trogons, once part of the virgin rainforest, have vanished.

Still, nature lovers will not go away disappointed. There are over 2,000 native plants and 170 species of ferns recorded. Soaring dipterocarp trees are a feature of this reserve. Don't expect to find the plants that feature in Singapore's urban greenery, though, as most of those are imported species. This is Singapore as she was in her earliest days.

The wildlife impresses with its variety. There are some 2 million insects and invertebrates, 660 types of spiders and 126 species of birds. Small animals like squirrels, anteaters, treeshrews, long-tailed macaques have survived too, although are infrequently seen. Don't be tempted to feed the monkeys. The forest provides for them sufficiently.

TRAILS

To visit Bukit Timah, wear comfortable clothing, sturdy shoes and scent-free insect repellent. The **Visitor Centre** (daily 8.30am–6pm) at the foot of the hill is a good place to start. Orientate yourself and check out the hiking routes clearly marked on the map at the entrance.

You will find maps and signs along the trails; you can get to the summit and back in under an hour or spend up to 3 hours covering more of the reserve.

The first part, straight up a paved road, can be disappointing, but once past this, you are in a primary rainforest complete with a heavy canopy at the uppermost layer, rattans and liana vines at mid-level, and red ginger flowers and dark purple bat lilies on the forest floor.

On leaving Hindhede Drive, take a taxi ride to the Rail Mall for lunch at **Galbiati**, see ①, or **Restaurant Home**, see ②

Food and drink

① GALBIATI

The Rail Mall, 400 Upper Bukit Timah Road; tel: 6462 0926; www.galbiati gourmet.com; Mon–Fri 11am–10pm, Sat–Sun 10am–10pm; $$

Italian chef-owner Roberto Galbiati helms this deli with freshly baked breads to go with hearty soups. Antipasti, pizzas and pastas are available too.

② RESTAURANT HOME

The Rail Mall, 392 Upper Bukit Timah Road; tel: 6456 1698; www.restauranthome.com. sg; daily noon–3pm, 6pm–11pm; $$

Feast on Peking duck barbecued with lychee wood alongside Singaporean heritage dishes such as hot stone chicken with lily buds.

At Singapore Zoo

MANDAI

Lush Mandai is the setting of the Singapore Zoo, where animals roam in naturalistic enclosures, and the one-of-a-kind Night Safari, where nocturnal wildlife prowl in the moonlight.

DISTANCE: Varies
TIME: Half a day
START: Singapore Zoo
END: Night Safari
POINTS TO NOTE: Take either bus no. 138 from the Ang Mo Kio MRT station or bus no. 927 from the Choa Chu Kang MRT station. The two attractions are located next to each other on Mandai Lake Road. If you plan to visit the Singapore Zoo, River Safari and Night Safari, get the Park Hopper multi-park ticket at a discounted package price. Aim to arrive at the Singapore Zoo in the morning, followed by River Safari to look at the pandas and then head over to the Night Safari at 6pm.

The Singapore Zoo and the Night Safari, known to be among the most thoughtful zoo settings in the world, provide an experience that will appeal to all. The 'open concept' of both zoos allows animals to roam freely in naturalistic habitats. Visitors are separated from most of the animals only by water moats and other low barriers.

SINGAPORE ZOO

The 26-hectare **Singapore Zoo ❶** (www. zoo.com.sg; daily 8.30am–6pm) is nestled in a rainforest and displays some 2,800 animals representing 300 species, 29 percent of which are threatened. There is a lot to see at the zoo, so this route features just the highlights.

A fruit bat in the Fragile Forest

Before you begin, note the animal show and feeding times posted at the entrance, so you can plan your tour. Recommended animal shows are **Elephants at Work and Play**, which features these mammals moving logs, and **Splash Safari**, with antics by sea lions and jackass penguins. The most spectacular feedings are at the polar bear and lion enclosures. There is also a tram service (separate charge) that plies the zoo.

Orangutans

The zoo has the world's largest colony of Bornean and Sumatran orangutans, the result of a successful captive breeding programme. See these primates up close at two free-ranging areas.

You can also have a **Jungle Breakfast with Wildlife** (daily 9–10.30am) in close proximity to orangutans as well as other creatures like snakes and otters at Ah Meng Restaurant (Terrace). Book one day in advance (tel: 6360 8560).

Other highlights

Explore rainforest ecosystems in the **Fragile Forest**, a re-created tropical jungle that is sanctuary to fauna as diverse as tamarins, lemurs, sloths, parakeets and butterflies.

The walkway leading to the **Tiger Trek** is so lush, you might even think you are in a tropical jungle. The exhibit is the habitat of the extremely rare Bengal white tigers.

Other themed areas worthy of your time include the **Great Rift Valley of Ethiopia**, where Hamadryas baboons dwell, the **Elephants of Asia**, reminiscent of the hills of Burma, and the **Australian Outback**, where kangaroos and wallabies prance around.

The latest attraction next to Singapore Zoo is **River Safari**. The highlight here is the two giant pandas from China which are on loan for a decade.

River Safari

In 2013, the zoo's parent company, Wildlife Reserves Singapore, introduced River Safari (80 Mandai Lake Road; www.riversafari.com.sg; daily 9am–6pm), Asia's first and only river-themed wildlife park, and home to over 5,000 animals. The highlight is the Giant Panda Forest housing the two resident giant pandas from China. Take a 'river adventure' down the Mississippi, Congo, Nile, Ganges, Murray, Mekong and Yangtze rivers, and visit the Squirrel Monkey Forest and Amazon Flooded Forest. This park also houses the world's largest freshwater aquarium.

Dinner and entertainment

After you are done with the zoo, move on to the Night Safari next door. For dinner, choose either **Ulu Ulu Safari Restaurant**, see ❶, or **Bongo Burgers**, see ❷. Another interesting dining option is the **Gourmet Safari Express** (tel: 6360 8560; daily 7–10pm), where you can dine and take in the animal exhibits at the same time in the comfort of a tram. Book at least one week ahead.

Getting up close with a giraffe   *Anteaters at the zoo*

NIGHT SAFARI

If you have been disappointed with disinterested animals in day zoos, it could be because 90 percent of tropical mammals are active only at night. At the 40-hectare (99-acre) **Night Safari ❷** (www.night safari.com.sg; daily 7.30pm–midnight;), the first night zoo in the world, animals are seen at their most active, feeding, socialising and prowling. The 41 naturalistic habitats are unobtrusively lit with a gentle moonlight glow so the animals are not disturbed. Some 2,500 animals representing 120 species, of which 29 percent are endangered, roam the Night Safari. The night zoo has also been successful in breeding endangered species such as the anteater, giant flying squirrel, Malayan flying fox and spotted hyena.

The Night Safari is extremely crowded at the weekend, so if you prefer a quieter visit, go on a weekday.

Themed exhibits

You can walk or travel around the eight themed exhibits, which are replicates of habitats found in Asia, Africa and South America, by tram (extra charge). The tram takes 45 minutes to complete the loop. As it moves along, your guide will point out the animals that come into view.

Noteworthy exhibits include the **Himalayan Foothills**, with highland goats and sheep; the **Indian Subcontinent**, where striped hyenas coexist with lions; and the **Nepalese River Valley**, home to the rhinoceros and the golden jackal.

Don't miss the **Asian Riverine Forest**, where you can find **Chawang**, the Night Safari's icon, standing at close to 3m (10ft) tall and weighing about 3,500kg (3.5 tonnes). The largest and heaviest among all the animals at both zoos, this beautiful elephant is a rare 'crossed tusker', with tusks more than 1m (3ft) long.

Walking trails

You can hop off at designated points along the tram route to divert on foot along four shorter trails: the **Fishing Cat**, **Leopard**, **Wallaby** and **East Lodge Trail** where you can see the majestic Malaysian tigers. The trails are clearly marked and rangers are stationed along the way to guide you.

Food and drink

❶ ULU ULU SAFARI
Night Safari; tel: 6269 3411; daily
5.30–11pm; $$
Try local cuisine like satay, fish tikka and
mee goreng (fried noodles) in an ethnic-
inspired setting.

❷ BONGO BURGERS
Night Safari; tel: 6269 3411; daily
5.30pm–midnight; $$
Dine on gourmet burgers, made with juicy
meat that is chemical- and preservative-
free. A Bornean tribal group entertains with
blowpipe and fire-eating demonstrations.

DIRECTORY

Hand-picked hotels and restaurants to suit all budgets and tastes, organised by area, plus select nightlife listings, an alphabetical listing of practical information and an overview of the best books and films to give you a flavour of the city.

Room at the Fairmont

ACCOMMODATION

Singapore has a huge range of accommodation from five-star hotels in the prime Marina Bay, Civic District and Orchard Road to smaller boutique hotels in atmospheric spots like Little India and Chinatown. The integrated resorts in Sentosa and Marina Bay have also sprouted a whole range of luxury hotels, with many leisure activities on offer.

In terms of accommodation, amenities and service standards, Singapore's top-end hotels easily compare with the best in the world. Deluxe, first-class and business-oriented hotels all have conference and business facilities, cable TV, IDD phones and high-speed internet access. No question, accommodation in Singapore is pricier than in some Southeast Asian cities, but there are many choices that suit all pockets.

An online hotel reservation system managed by the Singapore Hotel Association (SHA) can help you with last-minute bookings (www.stayinsingapore.com).

Price for a double room for one night without breakfast (not including the 10 per cent service charge and 7 per cent goods and services tax, except where noted):

$$$$ = over S$500
$$$ = S$350–500
$$ = S$150–350
$ = below S$150

The system provides real-time reservations and supply instant confirmation. SHA also has reservation counters at the arrival halls in Changi Airport's Terminals 1, 2 and 3 to assist you with bookings. When booking directly with the hotel, always ask if they have promotional rates and if breakfast is included. And be aware that the standard 10 percent service charge and 7 percent Goods and Services Tax (GST) will add significantly to the final rate.

Civic District

Carlton
76 Bras Basah Road; tel: 6338 8333;
www.carlton.com.sg; $$
This business-class hotel sits on a prime spot across from Chijmes and the Raffles Hotel. Choose from rooms in the Main Tower, Executive Wing or Premier Wing. Award-winning Cantonese restaurant and a bar and two cafés on site. A five-minute walk to the City Hall MRT station.

Fairmont Singapore
80 Bras Basah Road; tel: 6339 7777;
www.fairmont.com/singapore; $$$
Fairmont has 769 luxurious guest rooms and suites, with private balconies overlooking panoramic views of the harbour or the cityscape. The hotel also offers a long list of amenities and excellent restaurants, including Szechuan Court and Mikuni. Its Willow Stream Spa is perfect

A spacious Fairmont bathroom

for rejuvenating spa treatments. The City Hall MRT station is literally on its doorstep.

Hotel Fort Canning
11 Canning Walk; tel: 6559 6770; www.hfcsingapore.com; $$$
This colonial building was the British Far East Command Headquarters during World War II. Rooms are individually styled and there's also a gym, pool and Chinois Spa. Free internet access for all guests.

Hangout@Mt.Emily
10A Upper Wilkie Road; tel: 6438 5588; www.hangouthotels.com; $$
This funky backpacker's lodging is about a 10-minute walk from the Dhoby Ghaut MRT station. Rooms are clean but small and with few frills. A great place to meet other travellers.

Naumi
41 Seah Street; tel: 6403 6000; www.naumi hotel.com; $$$
A chic 73-room boutique hotel, the Naumi offers plush designer comfort, a 50-inch plasma TV, kitchenette and Wi-fi connectivity. An inviting rooftop infinity pool overlooks the city's skyline. The hotel's sixth floor is for ladies only. The City Hall MRT station is a convenient five-minute walk away.

...es
1 Beach Road; tel: 6337 1886; www.raffles.com/singapore; $$$$

The Grand Dame of historical hotels. Guests stay in suites and are cocooned in a private, genteel world where one is greeted by name and treads on wooden floors lined with antique rugs while gazing at museum-quality art pieces. The private pool is open 24 hours and bathrooms are designed for absolute indulgence. Across the road is the City Hall MRT station.

Swissôtel The Stamford
2 Stamford Road; tel: 6338 8585; www.swissotel.com; $$$
Once the world's tallest hotel until it was supplanted in 1999, this hotel sits above the City Hall MRT station and is practically part of a large shopping centre complex. There is a business centre, convention centre and a huge number of restaurants and bars (including the rooftop Equinox complex with fine dining Jaan restaurant), plus a luxurious spa and a well-equipped fitness centre.

Marina Bay

Conrad Centennial
2 Temasek Boulevard; tel: 6334 8888; www.conradhotels.com; $$$
This five-star has spacious and luxurious rooms with picturesque views of Marina Bay. It is an excellent choice for business travellers with its wide range of facilities and fine restaurants such as Golden Peony and Oscar's. The service staff are highly efficient. Convenient location for shopping, and only five minutes' walk to the Promenade MRT station.

The Fullerton
1 Fullerton Square; tel: 6733 8388;
www.fullertonhotel.com; $$$
Formerly the General Post Office, this historical jewel is now a luxury hotel. The colonnaded exterior gives way to a contemporary chic interior filled with Art Deco furniture. Amazing views from the 400 rooms and suites which either overlook the sunlit atrium courtyard, or have balconies that open out to panoramas of the city skyline, river promenade or Marina Bay. Raffles Place MRT station is five minutes away.

Fullerton Bay Hotel
80 Collyer Quay; tel: 6333 8388;
www.fullertonbayhotel.com; $$$$
An elegant hotel in a historic location that boasts stunning views of the Singapore skyline and bay. Exquisite touches include double-glazed floor-to-ceiling windows and Nespresso machines in all rooms. Have a meal at Clifford Pier followed by a nightcap at rooftop bar Lantern. A short walk to Raffles Place MRT.

Mandarin Oriental
5 Raffles Avenue; tel: 6338 0066;
www.mandarinoriental.com; $$$
Its plush rooms have floor-to-ceiling windows that overlook the city. It's well known for its eateries: Morton's, The Steakhouse, Cherry Garden Cantonese restaurant and the pool-side, Mediterranean-style Dolce Vita restaurant. The Promenade MRT station is five minutes' walk away.

Marina Bay Sands
10 Bayfront Avenue; tel: 6688 8888;
www.marinabaysands.com; $$$
Located in the massive Marina Bay Sands integrated resort, this hotel overlooks the city centre and bay area. Pick from nine types of rooms and suites. Among the many facilities in the complex are a stunning infinity pool, casino and shops, as well as trendy bars and clubs.

Marina Mandarin
6 Raffles Boulevard; tel: 6845 1000;
www.meritushotels.com; $$$
Apart from its spectacular atrium rising through 21 storeys, all rooms offer breathtaking views of Marina Bay, while premier rooms and suites are equipped with plasma TVs. The hotel's fine restaurants include Peach Blossoms for Chinese food and AquaMarine for Asian and international cuisine. Only a short walk to the Esplanade MRT station.

Pan Pacific Singapore
7 Raffles Boulevard; tel: 6336 8111;
www.panpacific.com/singapore; $$$
This hotel's 790 rooms and suites are contemporary and elegant, replete with beautiful views of the city or Marina Bay. It was the first hotel in Singapore to offer Wi-fi-operated mini-bars. Indian, Japanese and Chinese cuisines are available at its fine dining restaurants. The Promenade MRT station is a short walk away.

Ritz-Carlton Millenia
7 Raffles Avenue; tel: 6337 8888;

Sol LeWitt artwork adorns the atrium at Marina Bay Sands

www.ritzcarlton.com/hotels/singapore; $$$$

The sheer luxury hits you the moment you step into the foyer, with the contemporary design and marble-clad spaces studded with Dale Chihuly glass sculptures. Rooms are equally luxe but the pièce de résistance must surely be the oversized bathrooms with huge picture windows framing the large bathtubs. A less than five-minute walk to the Promenade MRT station.

Westin Singapore

12 Marina View, Asia Square Tower 2; tel 6922 6888; www.westin.com/singapore; $$$

Take a lift up to the level 32 of Westin Singapore and you will find the island's highest hotel lobby. Occupying levels 32 to 46 of the Asia Square Tower 2 at Marina Bay, this is Singapore's first integrated hotel situated within an office building. The hotel rooms promises dazzling views of the sea and the bay. Sink into the signature Heavenly Bed with its patented pillow-top mattress for a good night's sleep. To relax, take a dip in the infinity pool followed by a treatment at the Heavenly Spa by Westin™.

Singapore River

Gallery

1 Nanson Road; tel: 6849 8686; www.galleryhotel.com.sg; $$

Located in the Robertson Quay district, this 'design hotel' features post-modern architecture and lively, if rather strange,

décor, plus a variety of room sizes. The unique glass-sided pool is a definite highlight.

Grand Copthorne Waterfront

392 Havelock Road; tel: 6733 0880; www.grandcopthorne.com.sg; $$–$$$$

The rooms are nicely appointed and outfitted with wireless technology and Internet phones. The hotel also offers a long-stay option; La Residenza on the fifth and sixth floors comprises 24 luxurious studios, one- and two-bedroom units which come with kitchenettes.

Chinatown

Hotel 1929

50 Keong Saik Road; tel: 6347 1929; www.hotel1929.com; $$

Just outside the hubbub of Chinatown, this boutique property combines a mix of old-world Singapore architecture and nouveau chic style. No two rooms are the same and many are embellished with unique furniture from the owner's private collection. Its restaurant, Ember, which serves modern cuisine with an Asian twist, has a strong following.

Dorsett Hotel

333 New Bridge Road; tel: 6678 8333; www.dorsetthotels.com/singapore; $$

Located above Outram Park MRT interchange station, guests can explore Chinatown and surrounding areas easily and enjoy plenty of food and drink options in the vicinity. Rooms are modern and equipped with Wi-Fi and posturepedic mattresses. There's a landscaped roof garden and outdoor Jacuzzi to take a respite after all the sightseeing.

Link

50 Tiong Bahru Road; tel: 6622 8585; www.linkhotel.com.sg; $$

Billed as the biggest boutique hotel in Singapore, it features a contemporary design based on multicultural themes: Chinese, Indian Malay and modern. The hotel's prewar buildings, the Lotus and Orchid blocks, are connected by a unique bridge that spans across the bustling Tiong Bahru Road.

New Majestic

31–37 Bukit Pasoh Road; tel: 6511 4700; www.newmajestichotel.com; $$$

Local artists and designers had a hand in the interiors of the stylish and eclectic 30-room New Majestic. Each room has its own quirky character and features vibrant wall murals and claw-footed bathtubs. A highlight is its rooftop pool with glass portholes through which one can have a peek of what diners are eating at the New Majestic restaurant just below. Only a 2-minute walk to the Outram Park MRT station.

Parkroyal on Pickering

3 Upper Pickering Street; tel: 1800 255 7795; www.parkroyalhotels.com; $$$

This stunning contemporary hotel houses a luxurious spa, sprawling sky gardens and even a jogging track high above street level. The rooms, decked out in natural elements, offer views of the river and city.

The Scarlet

33 Erskine Road; tel: 6511 3333; www.thescarlethotels.com/singapore; $$

Located near Ann Siang Hill and Club Street, this 80-room boutique hotel is full of character. Its unabashedly gaudy interior is decked out in bold colours, and its five custom-designed suites each showcase a different personality. There is a gym, an open-air jacuzzi and a chic roof-top alfresco bar and restaurant overlooking Chinatown. The Chinatown MRT station is a 10-minute walk away.

Orchard Road

Four Seasons

190 Orchard Boulevard; tel: 6734 1110; www.fourseasons.com/singapore; $$$$

An intimate and elegant property with a marbled foyer, plush furnishings and exquisite artworks – about 1,500 Asian and international art pieces are on display. All rooms feature custom-designed beds, DVD and CD players with iPod docks, marble bathrooms with double vanity basins, deep-soaking tubs and luxuries such as Italian cotton bathrobes and Japanese yukatas. It is only a five-minute walk to the Orchard MRT station.

Goodwood Park

22 Scotts Road; tel: 6737 7411; www.goodwoodparkhotel.com; $$$

Goodwood Park's pool

This grand and graceful landmark exudes a strong colonial-era charm, with landscaped gardens that add a touch of serenity to the bustle of Orchard Road. It has 233 tastefully appointed rooms and suites complete with modern amenities, two outdoor swimming pools, a gym and four excellent restaurants, a deli and a bar. The Orchard MRT station is a three-minute walk away.

Grand Hyatt

10 Scotts Road; tel: 6738 1234; www.singapore.grand.hyatt.com; $$$$

A stone's throw from the Orchard MRT station, the Grand Hyatt impresses with its minimalist, almost stark decor and excellent service. The Grand Wing rooms are particularly lavish with soft linens and Bang & Olufsen sound systems. Dine at mezza9, where Sunday champagne brunch is a must.

Grand Park Orchard

270 Orchard Road; tel: 6603 8888; www.parkhotelgroup.com/orchard; $$

The hotel's location right in the middle of Orchard Road is highly convenient for shopaholics. The striking 'herringbone' design featured on its exterior glass facade is echoed throughout the hotel including the stylishly designed rooms.

Hilton Singapore

581 Orchard Road; tel: 6737 2233; www3.hilton.com; $$$

The city's longest-operating 5-star hotel, with a shopping arcade housing international fashion boutiques. Also conveniently located near shopping malls and 5 to 7 minutes' walk from Orchard MRT station. Fine-dining Western restaurant, as well as a bakery and café.

Hotel Jen Orchardgateway

277 Orchard Road; tel: 6708 8888; www.hoteljen.com; $$

This newest hotel along Orchard Road is touted as relaxed and friendly. The four-star accommodation located above Somerset MRT offers comfort and value. There's free wifi everywhere, with convenient mobile charging stations throughout the hotel. After your shopping spree, head to the rooftop leisure, wading or lap pool and enjoy superb city views. Food-wise, there's a restaurant serving local and international fare, as well as an on-the-go deli counter.

Mandarin Orchard Singapore

333 Orchard Road; tel: 6737 4411; www.meritushotels.com; $$$

With a fantastic location on Orchard Road, this swanky hotel offers 1,077 tastefully refurbished rooms and suites featuring in-room amenities such as flatscreen TVs, mini hi-fi systems and other bells and whistles. Premier rooms are equipped with sleek massage armchairs – perfect after a day's shopping. Two MRT stations (Orchard and Somerset) are within walking distance.

Marriott

320 Orchard Road; tel: 6735 5800;

www.singaporemarriott.com; $$$
The pagoda-roofed hotel at the corner of Scotts and Orchard roads is a well-known landmark with the Orchard MRT station at its doorstep. Its location is perfect for shopping and nightlife. There is a popular alfresco café, a Cantonese restaurant and a poolside grill. The famous Tangs department store shares the same building.

The Regent
1 Cuscaden Road; tel: 6733 8888; www.regenthotels.com; $$$
Expect spacious, well-appointed rooms and efficient service. It has an excellent Italian restaurant by the pool and fine dining Cantonese restaurant. Tanglin Mall is just next door and Orchard MRT station is a good 12-minute walk away.

Royal Plaza on Scotts
25 Scotts Road; tel: 6737 7966; www.royalplaza.com.sg; $$$
Located on Scotts Road (near Orchard Road MRT station), this hotel offers tastefully decorated contemporary rooms with generous work spaces and a complimentary in-room minibar, which is replenished daily. It is the first smoke-free business hotel in Singapore. Its lobby café, Carousel, features an international buffet spread and a gourmet deli filled with sweet treats.

St Regis
29 Tanglin Road; tel: 6506 6888; www.stregis.com; $$$$
St Regis brings its trademark style to a prime spot on Orchard Road. The design and furnishings are a bit over the top, but no one can fault its stupendous range of facilities: pool-side Italian restaurant, fine dining Cantonese, French brasserie, spa, swimming pool, business centre, private butlers for every room and a fleet of Bentleys to chauffeur guests around. The Orchard Road MRT station is a good 10-minute walk away.

Little India

Moon @ 23 Dickson
23 Dickson Road; tel: 6827 6666; www.moon.com.sg; $$
This is a no-fuss boutique hotel that's trendy, compact and comfortable. It's also close to Bugis MRT station, thus making it very convenient to get to any part of the city.

Parkroyal on Kitchener Road
181 Kitchener Road; tel: 6428 3000; www.parkroyalhotels.com; $$
Excellent-value hotel near Serangoon Road, next to the Farrer Park MRT station and opposite the 24-hour Mustafa Centre. Rooms are spacious and feature modern comforts. Facilities include a café serving Asian and Western food, Cantonese restaurant, executive floors, fitness centre and swimming pool.

Wanderlust Hotel
2 Dickson Road; tel: 6396 3322; http://wanderlusthotel.com; $$

Housed in an old school built in the 1920s, the concept of this hotel is incredibly unique. Each of the four levels was designed by award-winning local design agencies. The rooms are quirky and fun, albeit rather small. Its restaurant Cocotte dishes up hearty French fare.

Sentosa

Hard Rock Hotel Singapore

8 Sentosa Gateway, Sentosa Island; tel: 6577 8899; www.hardrockhotel singapore.com; $$$

Live it up like a rock star and get the legendary entertainment experience. Located within the Resorts World Sentosa integrated resort, it's ideal for visiting Universal Studios and exploring the rest of the island during your stay.

Mövenpick Heritage Hotel Sentosa

23 Beach View; tel: 6818 3388; www.moevenpick-hotels.com; $$$

This hotel is housed in a beautifully restored colonial building dating back to the 1940s. The restaurant offers reasonably priced buffet spreads and the World of Whisky lounge boasts a massive whisky collection. With the Imbiah Station (Sentosa Express) just directly opposite the hotel, guests can zip off to VivoCity in barely five minutes.

The Singapore Resort & Spa Sentosa

2 Bukit Manis Road; tel: 6275 0331; www.thesentosa.com; $$$

Stunning resort-style hotel located on a forested hill. Features both hotel-style rooms and suites as well as villas with private pools. Linked by a path directly to the beach. You may just want to park yourself at this idyllic retreat and not venture into the city. Be sure to book a massage at its adjacent So Spa, set in lush gardens.

Shangri-La's Rasa Sentosa Resort & Spa

101 Siloso Road; tel: 6275 0100; www.shangri-la.com; $$$$

Thanks to an S$80 million makeover, this resort now has upgraded guest-rooms and facilities. Not the most convenient place to stay for easy access to the city, but instead, the resort offers extensive recreational activities, from sailing to cycling. Restaurants here include Silver Shell Café, Trapizza and Barnacles, serving Mediterranean dishes and Asian-inspired specialities.

W Singapore – Sentosa Cove

21 Ocean Way; tel: 6808 7288; www.wsingaporesentosacove.com; $$$

Located next to Sentosa Cove's Quayside Isle, this trendy hotel attracts those who want to get away from the city. Partygoers will like the energetic vibe. Aside from the plush rooms, it has a modern grill restaurant, an international buffet restaurant, and a lobby bar with resident DJ. The poolside offers complimentary private cabanas equipped with iPad and iPod.

True Blue

RESTAURANTS

Singapore's cultural diversity has given the island-state an explosion of flavours – Chinese, Malay, Indian and Peranakan – that is entirely its own. Add to this the world's major cuisines, and you have a city that never stops eating.

There are few places in the world where life revolves around food like it does in Singapore. Singaporeans talk about food all the time. People from all walks of life can debate on where to get the freshest seafood or the best chicken rice for hours on end – preferably over a meal.

The racial mix of Chinese, Malays and Indians, as well as an expatriate population from the world over, has led to a range of cuisines. These immigrants brought their favourite dishes, ingredients and techniques, resulting in a variety of unique creations that are available today in venues ranging from hawker stalls to world-class restaurants.

It's also common to see Singaporeans making a beeline for buffets. Some of the best ones are located in upscale hotels and they serve a superb smorgasbord of international favourites plus decadent dessert and cheese spreads. Especially popular among expats is Sunday brunch with free-flowing champagne and luxurious foods such as oysters and lobsters.

Lately, fine dining has been undergoing a transformation of sorts, with restaurants offering more casual concepts such as grills, bistros and tapas, yet still featuring high-quality seasonal ingredients and fine techniques. The city has continued to attract many top-notch chefs in recent years. Boosting Singapore's reputation as an energetic gastronomic city are restaurants by celebrity chefs from Tokyo, Paris and New York. High-profile names such as Joel Robuchon, Tetsuya, Mario Batali and Daniel Boulud have all set up their outposts in Singapore thanks to the opening of the two integrated resorts, Marina Bay Sands and Resorts World Sentosa, in 2010. The island has embraced these culinary heavyweights with open arms and is expecting more to come.

Civic District

Garibaldi

36 Purvis Street, 01-02; tel: 6837 1468; www.garibaldi.com.sg; daily noon–2.30pm, 6.30–10.30pm; $$$$
Garibaldi is synonymous with Italian fine dining in the city. Helmed by well-known Chef Roberto Galetti, the kitchen

Price guide for a meal for one (excluding drinks and taxes):
$$$$ = over S$60
$$$ = S$40–60
$$ = S$20–40
$ = below S$20

Seafood and vegetable platter

DB Bistro Moderne's interior

uses only the best seasonal ingredients from Italy. His specialities include angel hair pasta with spiny lobster and a variety of robust risottos.

Kopi Tiam

2 Stamford Road, 2/F, Swissôtel The Stamford; tel: 6431 6156; www.swissotel.com/hotels/singapore-stamford/dining; Mon–Fri 11.30am–2.30pm, Sat–Sun noon–2.30pm, Mon–Sun 6–10.30pm; $$$

Make a beeline for tasty local dishes such as the Hainanese chicken rice, *rojak* and *laksa*. Get your spice fix with the collection of special curries such as Devil's curry, Vindaloo and Malay curry.

Mikuni

Level 3, Fairmont Singapore, 80 Bras Basah Road; tel: 6431 6156; www.fairmont.com/singapore/dining/mikuni; daily noon–2.30pm, 6.30–10.30pm; $$$$

Choose to sit at the teppanyaki, sushi or robatayaki counters where you can watch the chefs in action. Otherwise, opt for the main dining area where you can feast on the highly creative kaiseki menu featuring the best seasonal produce. The lunch bento sets are just as exquisite.

Shinji

1 Beach Road, 02-20 Raffles Hotel; tel: 6338 6131; www.shinjibykanesaka.com; Mon–Sat noon–3pm, 6–10.30pm; $$$$

This is the first and only outpost of two-Michelin-starred chef Shinji Kane-saka's famous Edomae-style sushi restaurant in Tokyo. Exquisite menus of perfectly executed sushi and pristine seafood are served. Watch the chefs prepare them right in front of you at the counter seats.

True Blue

47/49 Armenian Street; tel: 6440 0449; www.truebluecuisine.com; Tue–Sat 11.30am–2.30pm and 6–9.30pm; $$$

Located close to the Peranakan Museum, this eatery is adorned with the owner Benjamin Seck's personal collection of Peranakan antiques and artefacts. The dishes are just as impressive, but portions are small. Try the spicy beef *rendang* and *ayam buah keluak* (chicken stewed with black nuts).

Yhingthai Palace

36 Purvis Street; tel: 6337 1161; www.yhingthai.com.sg; daily 11.30am–2pm and 6.30–10pm; $$

This restaurant serves delightfully robust Thai cuisine. Must-tries include the papaya salad, deep-fried fish with mango sauce, string beans with shrimp, and for dessert, mango with sticky rice.

Marina Bay

DB Bistro Moderne

10 Bayfront Avenue, #B1-48 The Shoppes at Marina Bay Sands; tel: 6688 8525; www.dbbistro.com/singapore/; Mon–Fri noon–5pm, Mon and Sun 5.30–10pm, Tues–Sat 5.30–11pm, Sat–Sun 11am–5pm; $$$$

Pizza at Pizzeria Mozza

Located across the theatre, this contemporary American French bistro helmed by celebrity chef Daniel Boulud serves robust French fare created with flair. Its coq au vin and famous DB burger are must-tries. Brunch is served on weekends and a pre-theatre menu is available from 5.30pm to 7pm daily.

Hai Tien Lo

7 Raffles Blvd; 3/F, Pan Pacific Singapore; tel: 6826 8240; www.panpacific.com; daily 11.30am–2.30pm, 6.30–10.30pm; $$$
This fine Cantonese restaurant was relocated from the 37th floor to the third floor after the hotel's major renovation. The seafood dishes are always special, as is the signature barbecued Peking duck with pan-fried foie gras.

The Lighthouse

Level 8, The Fullerton Hotel, 1 Fullerton Square; tel: 6877 8933; www.fullertonhotel.com; daily noon–2.30pm, 6.30–10.30pm; $$$$
This small restaurant presents a fabulous fine dining Italian experience with stunning views. A great venue for romantic nights or special occasions. Well-executed Southern Italian cuisine covers dishes from regions like Campania, Sardinia and Sicily. The wine list is excellent too.

Pizzeria Mozza

10 Bayfront Avenue, #B1-42/46 The Shoppes at Marina Bay Sands; tel: 6688 8522; www.pizzeriamozza.com; daily noon–11pm; $$$
Pizzeria Mozza (adjacent to the finer Osteria Mozza) is celebrity chef Mario Batali's first venture into Asia. Mirroring his restaurant in California, this pizza joint filled with blaring rock music is lively and casual. There are two wood-burning ovens that churn out the most delicious pizzas in town.

Rang Mahal

3/F, Pan Pacific Hotel, 7 Raffles Boulevard; tel: 6333 1788; www.rangmahal.com.sg; daily noon–2.30pm, 6.30–10.30pm; $$$$
This elegant restaurant has been serving top-class Indian cuisine from the northern, southern and coastal regions since 1971. Dine on beautifully plated hot stone tandoori lamb chops or tandoor-grilled Portobello mushrooms with spices. A gourmet lunch buffet is available from Sunday to Friday.

Summer Pavilion

7 Raffles Ave; The Ritz-Carlton, Millenia; tel: 6337 8888; www.ritzcarlton.com/en/Properties/Singapore/Dining; daily 11.30am–2.30pm, 6.30–10pm; $$$
Flanked by a lush Chinese garden, Summer Pavilion is like a breath of fresh air. Feast on refined Cantonese dishes such as barbecued duck, fish noodles and flawlessly made dim sum.

Waku Ghin

Marina Bay Sands, 10 Bayfront Avenue, Level 2 Casino; tel: 6688 8507; www.marinabaysands.com/restaurants/

Waku Ghin　　　　　　　　　　　　*An elaborate sea urchin dish*

waku-ghin.html; daily 5.30pm and 8pm
(two seatings); $$$$

This is renowned chef Tetsuya Waku-da's first restaurant outside of Sydney. Enjoy top-notch European cuisine with Japanese influence using the freshest seasonal ingredients. The experience is highly personalised as you can talk to the chefs and watch them prepare your degustation meal right in front of you.

Singapore River

Absinthe

71/72 Boat Quay; tel: 6222 9068;
www.absinthe.sg; Mon–Sat noon–2.30pm,
5.30–10.30pm; $$$$

While French Chef François Mermilliod helms the kitchen, restaurant manager Vincent Jaureguiberry ensures that your dishes are well matched with fine wines. Dine on elegant French cuisine such as pan-fried foie gras with morello cherries and lobster bisque scented with cognac.

Ellenborough Market Café

Swissotel Merchant Court Hotel, 20
Merchant Road; tel: 6239 1848; daily
noon–2.30pm and 6.30–10pm; high tea
3.30–5.30pm; $$$

Overlooking the Singapore River, this restaurant is especially popular among locals who love the buffet spread of international and local favourites. Dine on chicken curry, satay, laksa, sushi and sashimi, then finish off with a plethora of desserts like coconut-based cendol and assorted Nonya cakes.

Kinara

57 Boat Quay; tel: 6533 0412;
www.thekinaragroup.com; daily 11.30am–
2.30pm, 6–11pm; $$

Dine by the Singapore River in a beautiful space decorated with antique furniture from Rajasthan. Warm, friendly staff serve cuisine from the North West frontiers of India. The signature roasted leg of lamb, marinated for over 24 hours, is a must-try.

Local Princess Terrace

403 Havelock Road, Lobby Level,
Copthorne King's Hotel; tel: 6318 3168;
www.millenniumhotels.com.sg; daily
noon–2.30pm, 6.30–10pm; $$

The Princess Terrace's is most famous for its authentic Penang-style buffet. Expect favourites such as *char kway teow* (flat rice noodles fried in sweet soy sauce), chicken curry, and delicious multi-coloured *Nonya* desserts – all prepared by experienced chefs from Penang.

Chinatown

Andre

41 Bukit Pasoh Road; tel: 6534 8880;
www.restaurantandre.com; Tues–Fri
noon–2pm, Tues–Sun 7–10pm; $$$$

The Bukit Pasoh enclave's hip quotient was raised when media darling chef Andre Chiang opened his highly anticipated restaurant here. Taiwanese-born Chiang has trained with some of the best French chefs, including Pierre Gagnaire, so you can expect only the

Cha kuay teow

finest southern French nouvelle cuisine here.

Bar-Roque Grill

165 Tanjong Pagar Road, 01-00; tel: 6444 9672; www.bar-roque.com.sg; Mon–Fri noon–2.30pm, 6–10.30pm, Sat 6–10.30pm; $$$$

Alsace-born Chef Stephane Istel, formerly of DB Bistro Moderne, set up this convivial restaurant and bar at the corner of Amara Hotel. Check out the massive rotisserie that churns out all kinds of delicious meats such as juicy free-range chicken and hefty pork knuckle.

The Blue Ginger

97 Tanjong Pagar Road; tel: 6222 3928; www.theblueginger.com; daily noon–2.30pm, 6.30–10.30pm; $$

This authentic Peranakan restaurant has been around for more than 10 years, satisfying customers with tasty offerings such as *ayam buah keluak* (stewed chicken with black nuts), beef *rendang* (dry beef curry) and the must-have durian *cendol* (a dessert with green jelly).

Buko Nero

126 Tanjong Pagar Road; tel: 6324 6225, Fri–Sat noon–2pm, Tue–Sat 6.30–9.30pm; $$$-$$$$

The menu reflects an Italian-Asian marriage – Venice-born Oscar Pasinato cooks while his Singaporean wife Tracy serves – with signatures such as tofu and vegetable tower, spaghetti with spicy crabmeat and prawns, and Horlicks ice cream. The tiny no-frills seven-table restaurant is always full. Call at least two weeks ahead for dinner reservations.

Burnt Ends

20 Teck Lim Rd; tel: 6224 3933; www.burntends.com.sg; Tue–Sat 11.45am–2pm, Mon–Sat 6pm till late; $$$$

At this modern Australian barbecue restaurant and bar, only the freshest produce is served. Sit at the bar counter and watch the chefs prepare your meal in the custom-made oven. Try the pulled pork burger and pickled quail eggs.

Gavroche

66 Tras Street; tel: 6225 8266; www.brasseriegavroche.com; Mon–Fri 11.30am–2.30pm, 6.30–10pm, Sat 6.30–10.30pm; $$$$

Located in a charming conservation shophouse, Gavroche is reminiscent of a typical Parisian brasserie. In fact, all the antique furnishings, including the bar, were hand-picked and shipped in from France. Chef Frédéric Collin showcases his grandfather's recipes in his classic French menu.

Majestic Restaurant

1/F, New Majestic Hotel, 31-37 Bukit Pasoh Road; tel: 6511 4718; Tue–Sun 11.45am–3pm, 6–10.30pm; $$$$

This stylish modern Cantonese cuisine offers signatures such as a combination of wasabi prawn, Peking duck and pan-seared foie gras as well as grilled rack of

Mooncakes   *It's easy to find tofu-based dishes for vegetarians*

lamb with Chinese honey. Diners get a view of the swimmers in the pool above through portholes in the ceiling.

Oso Ristorante

46 Bukit Pasoh Road; tel: 6327 8378; www.oso.sg; Mon–Fri noon–2.30pm, Mon–Sat 6.30pm till late. $$$$

Italian partners Diego Chariani and Stephane Colleoni run this popular restaurant located in a historic building in Bukit Pasoh. The restaurant has a separate cheese room and cigar room. Diego is famous for his regional Italian cuisine, including his home-made pastas.

Sabio

5 Duxton Hill; tel: 6690 7562; www.sabio.sg; Mon–Fri noon–late, Sat 5pm–late, Sun 11.30am–late $$$

This tapas bar serves authentic Spanish bites, oysters, sangria and wines. Head there early as it gets packed to the brim in the evenings, plus the bar subscribes to a no reservations policy.

Spizza for Friends

29 Club Street; tel: 6224 2525; www.spizza.sg; daily Mon–Fri noon–2.30pm, 6–10.30pm, Sat–Sun noon–10.30pm $$

Spizza's winning formula: ingredients imported from Italy, a thin and crispy crust and a wood-fired oven. Try the Quinta Pizza – tomato, mozzarella and black truffles topped with a cracked egg; or Isabella – mozzarella, parma ham and rucola (rocket).

Spring Court

52-56 Upper Cross Street; tel: 6449 5030; www.springcourt.com.sg; daily 11am–3pm, 6–10.30pm; $$

Established in 1929, this successful family-run restaurant in Chinatown is considered one of the oldest Cantonese restaurants in Singapore. Classics include crisp roast chicken, *popiah* (spring rolls) and golden cereal prawns. Dim sum is available for lunch.

Thanying

2/F, Amara Hotel, 165 Tanjong Pagar Road; tel: 6222 4688; daily 11.30am–3pm and 6.30–10pm; $$

This established restaurant serves authentic royal Thai cuisine. The green curry is excellent, as are the stuffed chicken wings and minced shrimp grilled on a stick of sugar cane and the fragrant olive rice. Be sure to leave room for the delicious dessert buffet.

Orchard Road

Basilico

2/F, Regent Hotel, 1 Cuscaden Road; tel: 6725 3232; www.regenthotels.com; daily 6.30–10.30am, noon–2.30pm, 6.30–10pm; $$$$

This restaurant by the pool offers alfresco and indoor dining. Aside from the à la carte menu, the outstanding antipasti buffet offers fresh seafood, salads, prosciutto ham with melon, and other Italian-inspired creations. The dessert selection, including Italian cakes, tarts and gelatos, is heavenly.

In Hua Ting

Chatterbox

Level 5 Meritus Mandarin, 333 Orchard Road; tel: 6831 6288; www.meritushotels.com/mandarin-orchard-singapore; Sun–Thu 11am–1am, Fri–Sat 11am–2am; $$

The iconic coffee house is most famous for its succulent chicken rice – it is expensive, but worth a try. The other local specialties such as *nasi lemak* (coconut rice with sambal and other condiments) and lobster *laksa* are great for those who like spicy dishes.

Crystal Jade Palace

04-19 Ngee Ann City, 391 Orchard Road; tel: 6735 2388; Mon–Sat 11.30am–11pm, Sun10.30am–11pm; $$

Crystal Jade is famous for its consistently good food. Feast on excellent roast meat and 'live' seafood such as the delicious baked prawns. The group also runs noodle and dumpling joint Crystal Jade La Mian Xiao Long Bao (tel: 6238-1661) in the same building.

Din Tai Fung

290 Orchard Road, B1-03/06 Paragon; tel: 6836 8336; daily 10am–11pm; $$

This popular restaurant is always crowded during meal times so queuing may be necessary. Feast on the famous *xiao long bao*, or steamed pork dumplings, and other delicious dishes such as the prawn wonton with chilli oil and wholesome chicken soup.

Hua Ting

2/F, Orchard Hotel, 442 Orchard Road; tel: 6739 6666; www.millenniumhotels.com.sg; daily 11.30am–2.30pm, 6.30–10.30pm; $$$

This elegant restaurant serves traditional and innovative Cantonese delicacies. Popular items include double-boiled shark's bone cartilage soup (a distinctive Chinese dish) with three treasures (stir-fried potatoes, green peppers and aubergine) and baked silver codfish with honey. The *dim sum* is also a highlight.

Imperial Treasure Nan Bei Restaurant

05-12/13/14 Ngee Ann City, 391 Orchard Road; tel: 6738 1238; www.imperialtreasure.com; Mon–Sat 11am–10pm, Sun 10.30am–10pm; $$

The Imperial Treasure restaurant empire is known for its consistently good food and prompt service. This outlet boasts top-grade Cantonese dishes, from roast goose to the comforting double-boiled chicken soup.

Les Amis

02-16 Shaw Centre, 1 Scotts Road; tel: 6733 2225; www.lesamis.com.sg; Mon–Sat noon–2pm and 7–9.30pm; $$$$

This sophisticated restaurant draws well-heeled diners with its exquisite French cuisine, which is light and contemporary with a focus on natural flavours. The award-winning wine list of some 2,000 labels is outstanding. The chic main dining room is illuminated by three antique Parisian chandeliers.

Fresh seafood at The Line

The Line

22 Orange Grove Road; Lower Lobby, Tower Wing, Shangri-La Hotel; tel: 6213 4275; www.shangri-la.com; daily 5am–1am; $$$$

The Line exudes loud, exuberant New York chic, thanks to the masterly touches of renowned interior designer Adam D. Tihany. Sixteen culinary stations serve a wide range of international cuisines – from aromatic tandoori chicken to fresh sashimi, all manner of seafood and a lovely dessert spread.

mezza9

10–12 Scotts Road, Grand Hyatt; tel: 6732 1234; www.singapore.grand.hyatt. com; daily noon–3pm, 6pm–11pm, Sunday brunch 11.30am–3pm; $$$$

This well-known restaurant features show kitchens for sushi, *yakitori*, seafood, Western and Chinese dishes as well as deli and dessert counters, walk-in wine cellar and a Martini bar. You can order from the various show kitchens and watch the chefs in action. The champagne brunch is especially popular.

One-Ninety

190 Orchard Blvd; Lobby Level, Four Seasons Hotel; tel: 6831 7250; www.four seasons.com/singapore; daily 6.30am–10.30am, noon–2.30pm, 6.30–10.30pm, all day dining 11am–10.30pm; $$$$

The open kitchen, communal dining and warm lighting set the stage for this lively restaurant. The small but scrumptious menu includes an amazingly juicy wood-fired steaks, seafood and pizzas.

Newton Food Cente

Bukit Timah Rd (near Newton MRT); daily lunch until late. $

Best visited at night. Ignore the touts, make sure you choose somewhere where prices are posted prominently, and you've got one of Singapore's best local food experiences. Good bets include barbecued seafood, grilled chicken wings, fishball noodles and fried carrot cake.

The Rice Table

02-09 International Building, 360 Orchard Road; tel: 6835 3783; www.ricetable.com. sg; daily noon–3.00pm and 6–9.15 pm; $

Diners love this place for its reasonably priced and substantial *rijstaffel* (rice table) buffet brought straight to the table. Indonesian dishes such as *tahu telor* (tofu omelette), beef *rendang* (spicy beef stew), grilled chicken and satay are firm favourites.

Straits Kitchen

Grand Hyatt Singapore, 10 Scotts Road; tel: 6732 1234; www.singapore.grand.hyatt restaurants.com/straitskitchen/; Mon–Fri noon–2.30pm, Sat–Sun 12.30–3pm, daily 6.30–10.30pm; $$$$

Local favourites are served buffet-style at this upscale restaurant. Take your pick from the Indian, Chinese and Malay theatre-kitchens where you can watch chefs whip up your dishes. Highly recom-

The White Rabbit is located in an old chapel

mended are the grilled *char kway teow* (fried rice noodles), tandoori chicken and satay.

Botanic Gardens and Tanglin Village

PS Café

28B Harding Road; tel: 9070 8782; www.pscafe.sg; Mon–Fri 11.30am–6.30pm, Sat–Sun 9.30am–6.30pm, Mon–Thu and Sun 6.30pm–midnight, Fri–Sat 6.30pm–2am; $$$

PS Café is a popular meeting place for the fashionable crowd. Lighter fare like salads and fish and chips are served at lunchtime, and more hearty offerings such as beef, mushroom and bacon ragout, and rosemary kofta curry are dished up for dinner. The cakes are scrumptious and the banana mango crumble is divine.

Samy's Curry

Blk 25 Dempsey Road; tel: 6472 2080; daily 11am–3pm, 6–10pm; $

A tenant at Dempsey Road's former civil service club before any of the other trendy outlets were opened, this 30-year-old restaurant specialises in fiery South Indian cuisine served on banana leaves. Signatures include the fish-head curry, masala chicken and prawns and Mysore mutton.

The White Rabbit

39C Harding Road; tel: 9721 0536; www.thewhiterabbit.com.sg; Tue–Fri noon–2.30pm, Sat–Sun 10.30am–3pm,

Tue–Sun 6.30–10.30pm; $$$$

This charming restaurant-bar is housed in a beautifully restored chapel. Tuck into classic European comfort food such as wild mushroom risotto or macaroni and cheese with truffle sauce and black truffle shavings, followed by black forest cake with a twist.

Little India

Muthu's Curry

138 Race Course Road; tel: 6392 1722; www.muthuscurry.com; daily 10.30am–10.30pm; $$

This restaurant serves a potent fish-head curry – its award-winning speciality – as well as South Indian dishes such as masala chicken and mutton chops cooked in tomato puree and spices – all served on banana leaves. Forget the cutlery and eat with your fingers.

Bukit Timah

Violet's Kitchen

881 Bukit Timah Road; tel: 6468 5430; www.violetoonskitchen.com;Tue–Thu 11.30am–10pm, Fri 11.30am–11pm, Sat 10.30am–11pm, Sun 10.30am–10pm; $$

Violet Oon, Singapore's culinary doyenne, runs this casual chic eatery with her son and daughter. Expect to feast on Violet's signature dishes which range from *laksa* to shepherd's pie via braised oxtail stew, not to mention a range of Nonya favourites.

Fish-head curry

Jumbo Seafood is very popular

East Coast

Guan Hoe Soon

38/40 Joo Chiat Place; tel: 6344 2761;
www.guanhoesoon.com; daily 11am–3pm,
6–9.30pm; $$

Singapore's oldest Peranakan restaurant was a mere coffee shop when it was founded in 1953 by an enterprising Hainanese man. You can't go wrong with traditional Straits Chinese dishes such as *satay babi* (pork *satay* curry), *ngo hiang* sausage and *ayam tempra* (chicken stew).

Jumbo Seafood

01-07/08, 1206 East Coast Parkway; tel:
6442 3435; www.jumboseafood.com.sg;
Mon–Sat 5pm–11.45pm, Sun noon–
midnight; $$$

Book in advance if you want to get a table. Outstanding dishes are the chilli crabs, pepper crabs and prawns sautéed with oat cereal, curry leaves and chilli. Ask for an alfresco table facing the sea.

Local East Coast Lagoon Food Village

1220 East Coast Parkway, next to car park
E2; daily lunch until late; $

At this atmospheric place, you can enjoy some of Singapore's best local food within a stone's throw of the sea. Make a beeline for the barbecue chicken wings, vermicelli with *satay* sauce and satay barbecue pork noodles. It is best visited at night when all the stalls are open.

PeraMakan

171 East Coast Rd, 01-02/03 Santa
Grand Hotel East Coast; tel: 6346 4202;
www.peramakan.com; Tue–Sun 11.30am–
3pm, 6–10pm; $$

Locals love the authentic, boldly flavour Nonya food served here. Owner-chef Kathryn Poh ensures that dishes are made using fresh ingredients. Try the beef *rendang* and home-made icy *chendol* dessert.

Red House Seafood

Block 1204 East Coast Parkway, 01-05; tel:
6442 3112; www.redhouseseafood.com;
daily noon–11.30pm; $$$

There are several highly popular seafood restaurants at the East Coast Seafood Centre along the East Coast Parkway. Red House is one of them, offering informal outdoor seafood dining. Dishes like chilli crab and drunken prawns are always fresh and lip-smacking.

Sentosa

Osia

Resorts World Sentosa, Crockfords
Tower, Level 2; tel: 6577 6560;
www.osiarestaurant.com; Thu–Tue
noon–3pm, 6–10.30pm; $$$$

Australian celebrity chef Scott Webster has created a menu inspired by fresh Aussie produce and Asian influences. Osia's signature dishes include the refreshing 'Seafood Ice Experience', butter poached lobster with mango salsa, and Valrhona hot chocolate soup.

NIGHTLIFE

Once dismissed as a sterile city with no soul, Singapore has undergone a remarkable transformation into a lively arts and entertainment hub. Whether it's a night of pub-crawling you're after or one of non-stop clubbing, the options are plentiful. There are chill-out alfresco bars set in lush gardens or on rooftops, chic lounges for the design-conscious, pubs with world-class bands, and dance clubs that rank among some of the best in the world.

Better known in international clubbing circles is Zouk, whose diehard fans continue to worship it as the ultimate in cool. Zouk plays a diet of edgy underground and house music, and has hosted in the past DJ luminaries. The annual ZoukOut, which began in 2000, is now touted as Asia's largest outdoor dance-music festival. This beach dance party held in December at Sentosa's Siloso Beach lures in throngs of clubbing fans.

Boat Quay might be considered just for tourists, but a fair amount of locals can be seen stumbling out of the bars here too. Many bankers from the CBD area throng these hotspots after work. Further along the river is Clarke Quay, which lures tourists to its restaurants, bars and dance clubs. Home-grown favourites at Clarke Quay are Attica/ Attica Too, where DJs spin everything from hip-hop to electronic dance.

Sentosa offers beachside party options, alongside cocktails and bites in a chill-out beach bar setting. The opening of the integrated resorts in 2010 has also added many vibrant nightlife options including Ku De Ta, perched on the magnificent Sands SkyPark, and Pangaea at the Crystal Pavilion.

Civic District

Loof
331 North Bridge Road; 03-07 Odeon Towers Extension Rooftop; tel: 6338 8035; www.loof.com.sg; Mon–Thu 5pm–1am, Fri-Sat until 3am; Happy hour Mon–Fri 5–8pm

This breezy alfresco rooftop bar offers some of the cheapest happy hour drinks in town (house pours are priced at $5 at 5pm, $6 at 6pm and $7 at 7pm). Pair refreshing Southeast Asian-inspired cocktails with the delicious local bar bites.

New Asia Bar
Level 71, Swissôtel The Stamford, 2 Stamford Road; tel: 9177 7307; www.equinoxcomplex.com; Sun–Tue 5pm–1am, Wed–Thu until 2am, Fri–Sat until 3am

A huge selection of cocktails and wines, and the best uninterrupted views of the city. City Space on the 70th floor is a classy bar with plush sofas and live jazz.

Boat Quay is a major nightlife hub

Marina Bay

Ku De Ta
SkyPark at Marina Bay Sands North Tower, 1 Bayfront Avenue; tel: 6688 7688; www.kudeta.com.sg; SkyBar noon till late daily, Club Lounge 11am until late daily, SkyDeck 10am until late daily, Poolside Terrace 8am–10pm daily

The stunning rooftop setting with the best views in town is a must-visit, whether you're after dining, drinking or just entertainment.

Lantern
80 Collyer Quay, The Fullerton Bay Hotel; tel: 6597 5299; www.fullertonbayhotel.com; Sun–Thu 8am–1am Fri–Sat until 2am

Lantern is an outdoor rooftop bar with great views of the marina and beyond. Sink into one of the curvaceous lounge chairs to sip champagne and indulge in gourmet snacks while a Cuban band plays in the background.

Pangaea
B2-05 Crystal Pavilion South, Marina Bay Sands, 10 Bayfront Avenue; tel: 6688 7448; www.pangaea.sg; Wed–Sat 10pm–6am

Make your way to the exclusive club via an underwater tunnel connected to The Shoppes at Marina Bay Sands. Resident and international DJs entertain party-goers at this Ultra-Lounge founded by Michael Ault.

Post Bar
The Fullerton Hotel, 1 Fullerton Square; tel: s6877 8135; www.fullertonhotel.com; daily noon–2am

This trendy bar serves a fine selection of martinis and signature cocktails. The ceiling and pillars of the former General Post Office have been incorporated into a sophisticated and modern interior.

Singapore River

Attica
01-03 Clarke Quay, 3A River Valley Road; tel: 6333 9973; www.attica.com.sg; Level 1 Wed 10.30pm–4am, Fri–Sat 10.30pm–4am, Level 2 Wed 11pm–5am, Fri–Sat 11pm–5.30am

Attica features a main bar, which is the focal point joining the dance floor to VIP spaces and a courtyard with a lush Balinese garden setting. Latino, jazz and funk is played at this sexy joint. Check out the alfresco bar on the 'lilypad' seats just by the river's edge.

Highlander Bar
01-11 Clarke Quay, 3B River Valley Road; tel: 6235 9528; www.highlanderasia.com; Sun–Thu 5pm–2am, Fri–Sat, public holiday evenings 5pm–3am

This bar recreates the atmosphere of a Scottish castle with wood panelling and barrelheads on a stone wall. A glass display lined with 200 types of whiskies is a sight to behold.

Molly Malone's Irish Pub
56 Circular Road; tel: 6536 2029; www.molly-malone.com; Mon 11am–midnight, Tue–Sat until 2am

A barman at work

A traditional bar that oozes quaint cosy charm, Molly Malone's is always busy with those inclined towards Irish-style dark beers.

The Penny Black

26/27 Boat Quay; tel: 6538 2300; www.pennyblack.com.sg; Mon–Thu 11.30am–1am, Fri –Sat until 2am; Sun until midnight

Popular with the financial district crowd, this pub serves great lunches of sandwiches and steaks, meat pies, and fish and chips – all washed down with English ales like Ruddles and Old Speckled Hen.

Zouk

17 Jiak Kim Street; tel: 6738 2988; www.zoukclub.com; Zouk open Wed, Fri–Sat 10pm–late, Phuture open Wed, Fri–Sat 9pm–late, Velvet Underground open Wed, Fri–Sat 9pm–late, Wine Bar open Tues 6pm–2am, Wed–Thu until 3am, Fri–Sat until 4am

This is one of Singapore's iconic clubs and has regular appearances by celebrity DJs. It also houses the chill-out Wine Bar and the more intimate Velvet Underground.

Orchard Road

Alley Bar

Peranakan Place, 180 Orchard Road; tel: 6738 8818; www.peranakan place.com; Sun–Thu 5pm–2am, Fri–Sat until 3am

A back alley was transformed into this hip hangout, which draws yuppies to its black terrazzo bar for cocktails such as mojitos and margaritas.

Balaclava

2 Orchard Turn, ION Orchard; #05-02; tel: 6634 8377; www.imaginings.com.sg; Mon 5pm–midnight, Tue–Thu until1am, Fri–Sat until 2am

This bar has great live music, a stylish crowd and an ultra-chic decor to match.

Brotzeit

313 Orchard Road, 01-27, Discovery Walk at 313@Somerset; tel: 6834 4038; Mon–Thu noon–midnight, Fri–Sat until 1am, Sun 11am–midnight

Brotzeit (German for 'bread time') gets crowded in the evenings, when expats and executives in the area come here for German beers and Bavarian bites.

Ice Cold Beer

9 Emerald Hill; tel: 6735 9929; www.emeraldhillgroup.com; Sun–Thu 5pm–2am, Fri–Sat until 3am

Occupying a shophouse built in 1910, this bar has ice tanks to ensure that its 50 types of beers are chilled to the right temperature in under 10 minutes. Its 9-inch hotdogs are incredibly good.

Martini Bar

10 Scotts Road, Grand Hyatt Singapore; tel: 6738 1234; http://singapore.grand.hyatt.com; daily noon–midnight

This incredibly popular bar adjacent to Mezza9 restaurant is famous for its variety of special martini concoctions

Spinning the decks   *Live music crowds*

(there are over 30 hand-crafted martinis in the menu). Bar bites such as
crab cakes are made using high-quality
ingredients.

Mink

GF Pan Pacific Singapore, 7 Raffles
Boulevard; tel: 6734-0305; http://theprive
group.com.sg

Sip champagne with jetsetters at this
luxurious club/lounge which offers private booths, dance podiums and premium.

Muddy Murphy's Irish Pub

111 Somerset Road; 01-02 TripleOne
Somerset; tel: 6735 0400; www.muddy
murphys.com; Mon–Wed 11am–midnight,
Thu and Sun until1am, Fri–Sat until 2am

One of the earliest Irish pubs to open in
Singapore, Muddy Murphy's continues
to thrive. In 1996, the bar was designed
and built to scale in Dublin, then dis-
assembled, shipped to Singapore and
reassembled. Enjoy live music and live
televised sports alongside pub grub,
Guinness and Kilkenny ale.

Pangaea

B2-05 Crystal Pavilion South, Marina Bay
Sands, 10 Bayfront Avenue; tel: 6688-7448;
www.pangaea.sg

Make your way to the exclusive club
via an underwater tunnel connected
to The Shoppes at Marina Bay Sands.
Resident and international DJs entertain party-goers at this Ultra-Lounge
founded by Michael Ault.

Azzura Beach Club Sentosa

46 Siloso Beach Walk; tel: 6270-8003;
www.azzura.sg

This entertainment, dining and hydro-
sports complex has a nightclub called
The Harem on the second level. Look
out for the line-up of international DJs.

Tanjong Beach Club

120 Tanjong Beach Walk; tel: 6270 1355;
www.tanjongbeachclub.com;
Tue–Fri 11am–11pm, Sat–Sun 10am–
midnight

A great place to unwind and party by the
beach. Check out the full moon party
held three times a year. Special cocktails feature local ingredients.

Wave House™ Sentosa

36 Siloso Beach Walk; tel: 63773113;
www.wavehousesentosa.com; 10.30am–
10.30pm

A simulated surfing, dining and lifestyle
venue where partygoers can enjoy live
music and late night parties at the two
beach bars. Enjoy music by top DJs, as
well as local and international acts.

South Singapore

St James Power Station

3 Sentosa Gateway; tel: 6270-7676;
www.stjamespowerstation.com

Three restaurants and nine entertainment spots vie for your attention here.
Pick one that suits your fancy – choices
include a dance club, chill-out lounge,
world music bar and more.

Children on a trip to Singapore Zoo

A–Z

B

Budgeting

Accommodation can cost anywhere from S$25 for a dorm room in a hostel and about S$120 for a room in a budget hotel to more than S$400 in a top-end luxury hotel. Food is cheap if you eat at hawker centres, usually about S$5, and so is public transport, less than S$2 per trip on the bus or train. Short taxi rides around the city centre will cost between S$8 to S$10.

If you live frugally, it's possible to survive on a budget of S$50 a day. If, however, you intend to live it up by eating out at good restaurants and checking out the city's nightspots, be prepared to budget about S$50 for a two- to three-course meal (without drinks), and S$30 for entry into the clubs (inclusive of one or two drinks). Drinks at bars are cheaper than at clubs, but the best deals are during happy hours, from about 5 to 8pm, when prices are reduced by between 20 and 50 percent on average. At other times, beer is priced from S$12 a pint and a glass of house wine from around S$14.

Set aside another S$30–40 per day for admission charges to attractions.

Business hours

Business hours are 9am–5pm Monday to Friday. Banks are usually open 8.30am–4pm on weekdays, and 8.30–1pm on Saturdays. Shops open from about 10am to 8pm daily (including Sunday) and many department stores are open until 9pm. Most Singapore Post branches in town are open from 8.30am to 5pm or 6pm on weekdays and from 8.30am to 1pm on Saturdays. Some Singapore Post outlets are open on Sundays too.

C

Children

Singapore is a safe place with plenty of family-friendly places. Some places in Singapore have attained the 'Pro-family Business' accreditation, such as the Singapore Zoo, Night Safari and several family-friendly malls. There are plenty of children's attractions, such as the Jacob Ballas Children's Garden at Botanic Gardens, Sentosa Island and those listed in the Western Singapore tour (see page 84). Children are usually given concessions on entrance fees.

Climate

As Singapore is located 137km (85 miles) north of the equator, the weather usually varies between hot and very hot. Temperatures range between 33°C (91°F) and 24°C (75°F), with high humidity levels from 64 to 98 percent. Most of the rain falls during the northeast monsoon between November and February and to a lesser degree during the southwest

A traditional shophouse

monsoon from May to September. Thunderstorms can occur throughout the year.

Clothing

Bring along light cotton wear and comfortable shoes for walking. Sandals and sunglasses are useful. Umbrellas and raincoats are always handy as downpours are unpredictable.

If you are planning a night out in town, bring along something dressier alongside proper shoes (not sandals or sportswear). You are welcome to step into the mosques and Hindu temples but before entering, remove your footwear. Note that mosques require that arms and legs be fully covered (by long-sleeved shirts, long pants and long skirts or sarongs) to enter. Sikh temples require visitors to wear a head covering, as do synagogues for males.

Smart-casual attire will see you through most occasions in Singapore. Dress to cope with the heat when outdoors and have a wrap or light cardigan for the sharp drop in temperature inside some air-conditioned buildings. Shorts and T-shirts are acceptable in many places, although many clubs and some restaurants have stricter dress codes.

Crime and safety

Singapore has one of the lowest crime rates in the world. Although it is generally a safe place, beware of pickpockets, especially in crowded areas. Place valuables in your hotel safe before heading out. It is generally safe for women to walk around alone, even at night.

Customs

Visitors carrying more than the equivalent of S$30,000 in cash or cheque have to declare this fact to the customs authorities upon arrival. Duty-free allowance per adult is 1 litre of spirits, 1 litre of wine or port and 1 litre of beer, stout or ale. No duty-free cigarettes are allowed into Singapore although they may be purchased on the way out. Duty-free purchases can be made both upon arrival and departure except when returning to Singapore within 48 hours. Passengers arriving from Malaysia are not allowed duty-free concessions.

The list of prohibited items includes drugs (the penalty for even small amounts can be death), firecrackers, obscene or seditious materials, endangered wildlife or their by-products, reproduction of copyright publications, video tapes, video compact discs, laser discs, records or cassettes, chewing tobacco and imitation tobacco products, cigarette lighters of pistol or revolver shape, and chewing gum (except dental or nicotine gum). For more information, contact **Immigration & Checkpoints Authority** (www.ica. gov.sg) and **Singapore Customs** (www. customs.gov.sg).

Disabled travellers

There is a growing awareness of the special needs of disabled people. The **National Council of Social Service** (tel: 6210 2500; www.ncss.org.sg) is a good information source. The **Disabled People's Association Singapore** (tel: 6899 1220; www.dpa.org.sg) has a booklet titled *Access Singapore*, which gives details of facilities for the disabled. Some of the newer buildings are designed with the disabled in mind but generally, getting around by public transport for the wheelchair-bound is a problem. There are some taxis that are large enough to accommodate wheelchairs but these have to be booked ahead.

E

Electricity

Electrical supply is on a 220–240 volt, 50 Hz system. Most hotels have transformers for 110–120 volt, 60 Hz appliances.

Embassies

Australia: 25 Napier Road, tel: 6836 4100
Britain: 100 Tanglin Road, tel: 6424 4200
Canada: 11-01 One George Street, tel: 6854 5900
New Zealand: 21-04, One George Street, tel: 6235 9966.
USA: 27 Napier Road, tel: 6476 9100.

Emergencies

Fire and ambulance: 995
Police: 999 (emergency), 1800-255 0000 (non-emergency)
Flight information: 1800-542 4422

Immigration & Checkpoints Authority: 6391 6100
STB Touristline: 1800-736 2000
Directory assistance: 100 (or 161 from public phone)

Etiquette

Most good behaviour in Singapore is law-enforced; public signage is usually very good and there are clear signs explaining what to do and what not to do.

Road crossing: Pedestrians must use a designated crossing if one is available within 50 metres (165ft), or else risk a fine of up to S$1,000 for jaywalking.

Littering: The government has taken great pains, not only to keep Singapore's streets clean, but also to inculcate civic-conscious habits in locals. Litter bins are found everywhere. First-time offenders are fined S$300 (be it a bus ticket, a cigarette butt or a sweet wrapper).

Toilets: Failure to flush urinals and water closets after use in public toilets (hotels, shopping complexes, etc) can result in a S$150 fine. To date, no one has ever been convicted of this offence. Still, take no chances.

Chewing gum: Contrary to belief, you won't go to jail for chewing gum. The ban covers only the sale and importation of chewing gum, not the actual act of gum-chewing. Note: A law passed in 2003 allows the sale of gum with therapeutic value, for instance, nicotine-laced gum to help smokers kick the habit. These items can only be bought from the pharmacist, not off the shelves.

Chinese temples are less formal than other religious houses

Public transport: No eating, drinking or smoking is allowed aboard buses and MRT trains. And passengers are banned from carrying smelly durians on board MRT trains too!

Religious and cultural habits: When keeping company with Muslims and Hindus, you should be careful neither to eat nor offer anything with your left hand. Remove your shoes before entering a mosque or an Indian temple. More informal styles prevail at Chinese temples. Visitors are most welcome to look around at their leisure and stay for religious rituals, except in some mosques. While people pray, it is understood that those not participating in the service will stand aside. Ask permission before taking photographs: the request is seldom, if ever, refused. Modest clothing is appropriate. Most temples and mosques have a donation box for funds to help maintain the building. It is customary for visitors to contribute a token amount.

F

Festivals

Although the dates of ethnic festivals vary because they are based on the lunar calendar, most are confined to one or two specific months of the year. The only exception is the Muslim festival of Hari Raya Puasa, which advances by a month or so each year. The other major Muslim festival is Hari Raya Haji, which marks the sacrifices made by Muslims who make the pilgrimage to Mecca.

January/February

Lunar New Year is the most important festival for the Chinese. A colourful parade called **Chingay** is held, with cultures from all over the world celebrated. Also during this period is the Indian harvest festival of **Ponggal**. Then comes the Indian festival of **Thaipusam** where devotees perform acts of penance.

March/April

Good Friday, which precedes Easter, is observed at many Christian churches in Singapore. Also around this time the Chinese observe **Qing Ming** in remembrance of deceased ancestors and loved ones.

The **World Gourmet Summit** and **Singapore Film Festival** are also held during these months.

May/June/July

Vesak Day (May) commemorates Buddha's birth, enlightenment and death. The **Dragon Boat Festival** (June) is held in remembrance of the poet Qu Yuan, who drowned himself in protest against political corruption in China. The annual **Singapore Arts Festival** (May/June) brings top-rate performers from around the world. The **Great Singapore Sale** (end May to mid July) is an island-wide shopping extravaganza. The **Singapore Food Festival** is held in July.

August/September

To celebrate **National Day** on 9 August, a parade and mass displays are held at the Marina Bay Floating Stadium. The

Mooncake Festival coincides with what is believed to be the year's brightest full moon during the eighth lunar month.

October/November/December
The most important Hindu festival **Deepavali** is in October/November. **Zouk-Out**, an annual dance party is held at Sentosa's Siloso Beach. Orchard Road lights up for **Christmas**, and the year winds up with carols sung in the streets.

G

Gay and lesbian travellers

Engaging in homosexual activity is an offence, but it does not mean it is non-existent. In general Singapore society is still fairly conservative when it comes to public displays of gay affection, and these actions are likely to draw stares. But that is about as much reaction as you will get as Singaporeans do not usually react aggressively to homosexuality. The unofficial gay hangout is Tanjong Pagar, where the majority of the gay bars are located. Singapore's gay websites are www.fridae.com and www.utopia-asia.com.

H

Health

Singapore has no free medical care, so be sure you are covered by insurance. Most hotels have doctors on call. The local water from the tap is treated and safe for drinking. Strict control is exercised over the hygiene of food sold, from hawker stalls to hotels. If you require treatment, there are more than 20 government and private hospitals as well as umpteen number of clinics for any eventuality. Singapore is fast gaining a reputation as a regional medical hub par excellence; the number of foreigners seeking treatment here is high. Consultation fees start from about S$30 in a private practice.

Hospitals
Mount Elizabeth Hospital: 3 Mount Elizabeth; tel: 6737 2666; www.mountelizabeth.com.sg
Raffles Hospital: 585 North Bridge Road; tel: 6311 1111; www.rafflesmedical.com
Singapore General Hospital: Outram Road; tel: 6222 3322; www.sgh.com.sg

Pharmacies
These are open 9am–9pm. **Guardian's** pharmacies have in-house pharmacists. It is wise to travel with your own prescriptions and medications.

I

Internet

Wireless@SG is a scheme that provides free wireless connection at selected hotspots. You will need a mobile device with Wi-fi facility and will need to register online with a service provider: M1 (tel: 6655 5633; www.m1net.com.sg/Wireless-SG), Starhub (tel: 6873 2828; www.starhub.com/wsg), **Singtel** (tel: 1688; www.singtel.com/wirelessSG) or Y5ZONE (tel: 6491 9652; www.y5zone.

Chingay parade

sg). Check the **Infocomm Development Authority** website (www.ida.gov.sg) for the locations of all the hotspots.

L

Left luggage

Bags can be stored at the Changi Airport's Left Baggage counters at Terminal 1 (tel: 6214 0318), Terminal 2 (tel: 6214 0448/1683) and Terminal 3 (tel: 6242 8936/6214 0672). Alternatively, check with any of the airport's information desks. Charges for the first 24 hours start at S$3.21 for cabin bags, S$4.28 for suitcases and S$8.56 for odd-sized items.

Lost property

To lodge a police report, visit the nearest police station or call 1800-255 0000. For lost items on SMRT buses and trains, call 1800-336 8900.

For taxis, call the respective operators. For lost luggage at the airport, call 6511 0459 (Terminal 1 and 2), 6247 5714 (Terminal 3).

M

Maps

Maps are available at the Changi Airport and the Singapore Tourism Board's office at Tourism Court, 1 Orchard Spring Lane; tel: 6736 6622, as well as at the Singapore Visitors Centre at the junction of Orchard and Cairnhill Roads.

Insight Guide Fleximap: Singapore is a handy, laminated map that won't break in the rain, should one of Singapore's tropical downpours strike!

Media

Newspapers: *The Straits Times* and *The Business Times* are local English-language dailies with local and international news. The New Paper, a tabloid, is published in the morning and afternoon. *Today* is available free at MRT stations. Foreign newspapers like the *International Herald Tribune*, *Financial Times* and *Asian Wall Street Journal* are available on the day of publication at major business hotels and large bookshops.

Radio: English-language channels are Gold FM (90.5 mhz), Symphony 92 FM (92.4 mhz), News Radio 938 (93.8 mhz), 987 FM (98.7 mhz); Class 95 FM (95 mhz); Radio 91.3 (91.3 mhz); and Power 98 (98.0 mhz). The BBC World Service is on 88.9 mhz.

Television: Local TV stations broadcast via the following channels: Channel 5 in English, Channel 8 and Channel U in Mandarin; Suria in Malay; Vasantham in Tamil; Okto shows kids programmes as well as documentaries and arts content and Channel NewsAsia broadcasts news and current affairs programmes. Cable is available through Starhub Cable TV, which operates 24 hours.

Minimum age

To buy and consume alcohol and cigarettes, a person has to be 18 years old. The minimum age allowed in dance clubs is usually 18 for ladies and 23 for men.

It's easy to find newspapers and magazines

Some clubs allow anyone aged over 18 to enter.

Money

The local currency consists of notes in $2, $5, $10, $50, $100, $500, $1,000 and $10,000 denominations. Coins are in denominations of 5, 10, 20, 50 cents and $1. Licensed moneychangers found in shopping malls offer the best rates. International charge and credit cards are widely accepted. Besides banks, there are ATMs in shopping centres, MRT stations, and at some major tourist attractions. Traveller's cheques can easily be encashed in most of the banks. Most large shops accept traveller's cheques in lieu of cash after conversion of the prevailing rate of exchange.

Tipping: Most hotel and restaurant bills come with a 10 percent service charge on top of a 7 percent Goods and Services Tax (GST). Tipping is not expected, but is appreciated in cases of special effort.

Taxes: A GST of 7 percent is charged on most purchases, which is refundable for visitors who make purchases from shops participating in the **Global Blue** and the **Premier Tax Free Scheme**, which display 'Tax Free Shopping' and 'Premier Tax Free' stickers respectively. The refund applies to purchases exceeding S$100. The Electronic Tourist Refund Scheme (eTRS) has replaced the paper refund form system. Choose a credit or debit card to be used as an eTRS Token for linking up all your entitled purchases with a refund. With this token, you will be able to retrieve all your purchases at one time. All you then have to do is apply for your GST refund claims using the eTRS self-help kiosk at the airport. Retailers will give you an eTRS ticket at the point of purchase and, even if you don't use a credit or debit card as an eTRS token, you can still use this ticket to apply for your refunds at the airport kiosks.

Postal services

Postal services are fast and efficient. Most hotels will handle mail for you or you may post letters and parcels at any post office. The **Singapore Post** branch at 1 Killiney Road is open Mon−Fri 9.30am−9pm, Sat 9.30am−4pm, and Sun and public 10.30am−4pm; the branch at the Changi Airport's Terminal 2 is open 8am−9.30pm daily. Call 1605 or check www.singpost.com.sg for more information about postal rates, express mail and other services, including its courier service called SpeedPost.

For other international courier services, check **DHL Express'** website at www.dhl.com.sg (or call 1800-285 8888), or **FedEx** at www.fedex.com.sg (or call 1800 743 2626).

Public holidays

New Year's Day: 1 January
Chinese New Year: January/February
Good Friday: April
Labour Day: 1 May
Vesak Day: May

Getting inspiration at a photography exhibit

National Day: 9 August
Deepavali: October/November
Christmas Day: 25 December
Hari Raya Puasa: date varies
Hari Raya Haji: date varies

Smoking

Smoking is not allowed at all enclosed public places like restaurants, museums, theatres, cinemas, shopping malls and government offices – in short almost everywhere in Singapore! The penalty for a smoking offence is up to S$1,000. Some restaurants have alfresco sections with designated smoking areas, and many bars and clubs have enclosed rooms reserved for smokers. Several hotels are now fully smoke-free but most still have smoking rooms or entire floors.

Telephones

The country code for Singapore is 65 (there are no area codes). To call overseas from Singapore, dial the international access code 001 or, for cheaper calls, either 013 or 019, followed by the relevant country code.

Mobile phone users with global roaming access should take note that the local network is GSM, common to most countries except Japan and the USA. To keep your costs down, buy a local SIM card from one of the three service providers: **Singtel** (tel: 1626 or 6738 0123),

M1 (tel: 1627 or 1800-843 8383) or **Starhub** (tel: 1633 or 6825 5000). These cards, which give you a local mobile number, cost a minimum of S$20 and can be topped up when the value falls. All local mobile numbers begin with an '8' or '9'.

Coin-operated public phones are a rare sight in Singapore, given the high saturation levels of mobile phones. Post offices are your best bet; some phones here can be used for worldwide calls. For convenience, buy S$3, S$5, S$10, S$20 or S$50 phone cards for both local and overseas calls. Local calls cost 10 cents for every 3 minutes.

Tourist information

There's a wealth of free literature at the airport, hotels, shopping centres and tourist attractions. Your hotel concierge is also a good source of information.

The **Singapore Tourism Board** (24-hour infoline: 1800-736 2000; www.yoursingapore.com) operates several visitor centres. The most useful location is the **STB Visitors Centre** at the junction of Cairnhill Road and Orchard Road (daily 9.30am–10.30pm), just opposite the Somerset MRT station. Other STB Visitor Centres are found at ION Orchard and Kreta Ayer Square in Chinatown.

Tours

Trishaws: Although mainly used by tourist groups, you can hire a trishaw on your own. Just make sure you agree on the destination and fare before starting out.

A tour of the city, lasting approximately 30 minutes, will cost S$39. Contact **Trishaw Uncle** (tel: 6337 7111; www.trishaw uncle.com.sg) for more information.

SIA Hop-On: This is a tourist bus service that operates unlimited rides to the various attractions in the city from 9am to 9pm daily. It stops at major hotels, shopping malls and landmarks. Pay $25 ($8 for Singapore Airlines and SilkAir passengers) and you can start your tour at your own time. Each ticket is valid for 24 hours. (tel: 6338 6877; www.siahop on.com)

HiPPO City Tours: You can purchase a one- or two-day **Singapore Sightseeing Pass** from the **DUCK & HiPPO Group** (tel: 6338 6877; www.ducktours.com.sg). With this pass, you have unlimited access to five City HiPPOtours; each tour travels a themed route and takes you to key districts and attractions around the island. The tours come with live commentary and you have the option of hopping on and off at any time and anywhere. The company also offers a two-day **Singapore Pass**, which combines 15 tours and attractions, including the popular DUCKtours.

Boats: A cruise on a bumboat is a novel way of taking in the sights along the Singapore River. Operated by **Singapore River Cruises** (tel: 6336 6111; www. rivercruise.com.sg), the Singapore River Experience A Tale of 2 Quays is a 40-minute cruise ($22) that takes in Boat Quay, Clarke Quay and Marina Bay. There's also a Marina Bay Laser Show Cruise ($30) that departs at 7.45pm.

Themed tours

RMG Tours (tel: 6220 8722), **Singapore Sightseeing** (tel: 6336 9011), **SH Tours** (tel: 6734 9923) and **Holiday Tours** (tel: 6738 2622) operate half- and full-day tours. Apart from the usual tours, these companies also operate themed tours that focus on cuisine, *feng shui* (Chinese geomancy), colonial history and other aspects of Singapore.

Journeys' Original Singapore Walks (tel: 6325 1631; www.singaporewalks. com) has walking tours to places like Little India, Chinatown, Kampong Glam and the Civic District. Its Changi Museum War Trails is a coach tour that focuses on World War II Singapore.

Time zone

Singapore is 8 hours ahead of GMT.

Transport

Getting there

By Air: Changi Airport (www.changi airport.com; tel: 1800-542 4422 for flight information; tel: 6542 9727 (Terminal 1), 6542 9792 (Terminal 2), 6307 8555 (Terminal 3), for customer service) is consistently named the world's best airport by travellers and businessmen. There are work spaces for laptops, business centres, an airport hotel, gym, and more; improvements and new facilities are constantly being added. There are three terminals – Terminal 1 (T1), Terminal 2 (T2), Terminal 3 (T3).

All three terminals offer a large assortment of duty-free shops, food outlets,

Ornate Chinese temple details

bars and entertainment options. Passengers can also shuttle between T1, T2 and T3 by the **Sky Train** service (daily 5am–2.30am).

Changi Airport is linked directly to 270 cities in 60 countries, with 100 airlines operating over 6,600 flights a week. The award-winning **Singapore Airlines** (www.singaporeair.com) flies to more than 60 cities in over 30 countries and its sister airline **SilkAir** (www.silkair.com) serves 34 destinations in Asia.

By Sea: Most visitors on a cruise arrive at the **Singapore Cruise Centre** (tel: 6513 2200; www.singaporecruise.com) located at the HarbourFront Centre. Singapore-based cruise liners sail to various countries in the region and also offer one-way cruise options. Contact **Star Cruises** (tel: 6223 0002; www.starcruises.com) for more information.

Tanah Merah Ferry Terminal (tel: 6545 2048), located near Changi Airport, has ferry services to Bintan and Batam islands in Indonesia and also to Tioman island in Malaysia.

By Road: Singapore is accessible by road from Ipoh and Kuala Lumpur on the west coast, and Kota Bharu on the east. It takes about 5 hours to drive from Kuala Lumpur (KL) via the North-South Highway. Travelling via Johor Bahru, entry into Singapore is either through the Woodlands Checkpoint in the north of Singapore or the Tuas Second Link in the west. Several private bus companies and travel agents in Singapore operate air-conditioned bus services to Malaysia and southern Thailand. **Transtar Travel** at 01-12 Golden Mile Complex, 5001 Beach Road, has frequent daily departures and tickets can be booked online (tel: 6299 9009; www.transtar.com.sg).

By Rail: A railway line links Singapore to KL, Butterworth and Bangkok, as well as to Tumpat, near Kota Bharu. Enquire at the **Woodlands Train Checkpoint** (tel: 6767 5963; www.ica.gov.sg.)

The **Eastern & Orient Express** has a luxury train that travels the 1,900km (1,200-mile) route linking Bangkok, KL and Singapore (tel: 6260 9495; www.orient-express.com).

Getting around

From the airport: There are several easy ways of getting to town from the airport.

The taxi stands at the Changi Airport are well organised. The 20-minute trip (barring peak-hour traffic) to the city on the East Coast Parkway (ECP) costs about S$25, including surcharges.

If you wish to travel in style, book a premium Limousine Taxi at a flat rate of $55 per departure from the airport. For larger groups, a 7-seater Maxicab costs a flat rate of $60 per departure from the airport.

The Airport Shuttle operates air-conditioned 9-seater coaches which serve all major hotels except those in Changi and Sentosa. Buy tickets at the Ground Transport Desk of all terminals. Tickets cost S$9 (adult) and S$6 (child), and the bus departs every 15 minutes from 6am–9pm and 5pm–1am, and 30 minutes at other times of the day.

Sightseeing tour bus in Little India

The train ride from the airport to the City Hall MRT station downtown, with a transfer at the Tanah Merah MRT station takes about 30 minutes. The train ticket costs S$1.90.

The airport is also served by air-conditioned public buses, the stands for which are located in the basements of T1, 2 and 3. Bus no. 36 takes you direct to the city. The ticket costs below S$2 and exact change is required.

Taxis: The easiest way to see Singapore is by taxi. There are more than 23,000 taxis plying the roads and most drivers speak or understand English. Within the CBD (and Orchard Road), taxis must be boarded and alighted at taxi stands or on side roads. Elsewhere, simply flag one down on the street. During peak hours, or when it is raining, booking a taxi is the best option. Call tel: 6342 5222, or the individual taxi companies: **Comfort/CityCab** (tel: 6552 1111), or **SMRT** (tel: 6555 8888). Flag-down fare starts from S$2.80 to S$3.20 for the first kilometre, depending on the type of taxi you get. Most taxis accept credit cards.

A slew of surcharges apply: advance bookings, Electronic Road Pricing (ERP), midnight (midnight–6am), extra baggage, peak-hour; airport surcharge for taxis that depart from the airport.

Cars: Avis (tel: 6737 1668) and **Hertz** (tel: 1800-734 4646) offer both self-drive and chauffeur-driven cars. You will need an international driver's license. Driving is on the left and seat belts are compulsory. Also, you must understand the **Electronic Road Pricing** (ERP) system before you drive. During peak hours, the ERP scheme controls traffic flow into the Central Business District and on major expressways. There is a scale of charges applicable to different periods and vehicle types. Charges are indicated on electronic boards just before an ERP gantry. When you drive through an ERP gantry, it will automatically deduct the correct fee from the cash card inserted into a special gadget in your car. Pre-paid cash cards are available at post offices or petrol stations; most car rental companies will also sell you one.

Buses: Efficient bus services operated by **SBS Transit** and **SMRT** cover most of the island and operate from 6am–midnight. Fares are S$0.80 to S$1.50 for non-air-conditioned buses and S$0.90 to S$1.80 for air-conditioned buses.

Be sure to have the exact fare as bus drivers do not give change. For convenience, buy a S$15 **ez-link card** which is inclusive of S$5 card cost (non-refundable), S$3 travel deposit and S$7 stored value. This allows cashless payment on all public buses and the MRT. By using the ez-link card, commuters can also enjoy lower fares and rebates when transferring between trains and buses.

Tap your ez-link card on the electronic reader located at the bus entrance (or turnstile at the MRT station), which then automatically deducts the maximum fare. When alighting from the bus or disembarking from the train, tap the card again on the reader at the exit, and the

Shoppers on Orchard Road

unused fare portion will be credited back into the card.

Ez-link cards are sold at Transitlink offices at all MRT stations and bus interchanges. You can top it up at these same offices. For information on ez-link cards and concession passes, visit www.transitlink.com.sg.

An alternative is the **Singapore Tourist Pass** (www.thesingaporetouristpass.com.sg), which gives visitors unlimited rides on Singapore's MRT, LRT and bus services. 1-day (S$10), 2-day (S$16) and 3-day (S$20) tickets are available (with a S$10 refundable deposit) and can be bought at selected MRT stations. This pass comes with a free copy of the '**Travel with Ease – Public Transport Guide for Tourists**' guide, which contains useful information on the various modes of public transport and gives travel directions to various sights and attractions. The guide is available free at Singapore Visitors Centres and selected MRT stations.

MRT: The efficiency of the city's metro system, known as the **Mass Rapid Transit** (MRT) (www.smrt.com.sg) draws the envy of commuters everywhere. Altogether, there are 86 stations on the East-West and North-South and Circle lines. SBS Transit (www.sbstransit.com.sg) operates the North East Line, which has 16 stations, and the new Downtown Line which is opening in three stages (2013, 2016 and 2017) will have a total of 24 stations when complete. The Downtown Line will be the longest underground and driverless MRT line in Singapore.

Trains operate around 5.15am–12.49am and fares are S$0.90–1.90. Trains run at intervals of 2–8 minutes depending on the time of travel.The price of a single-trip ticket dispensed by ticket machines include a S$1 deposit. This is refunded by the ticket machine at the end of your trip. This can be a bother, so if you plan to use buses and the MRT for several trips, buy a stored-value **ez-link card** or the **Singapore Tourist Pass**. Tap your card on the electronic readers at the start and end of your trip as you do on buses.

Toilets

Singapore's toilets are some of the cleanest in the world. In shopping malls, there are washrooms on every floor and in tourist attractions there are ample toilets for the convenience of visitors. The majority of the toilets are very well-maintained except for some old buildings and hawker centres. Note: you may have to pay a 20-cent fee to enter some public conveniences in Singapore.

Visas and passports

Visa requirements can vary, so check with a Singapore embassy or consular office in your home country. Most visitors are given a 30-day social visit pass on arrival. Application for renewals can be made online or at the **Immigration & Checkpoints Authority** (ICA), 10 Kallang Road. For details, call the hotline: 6391 6100; www.ica.gov.sg.

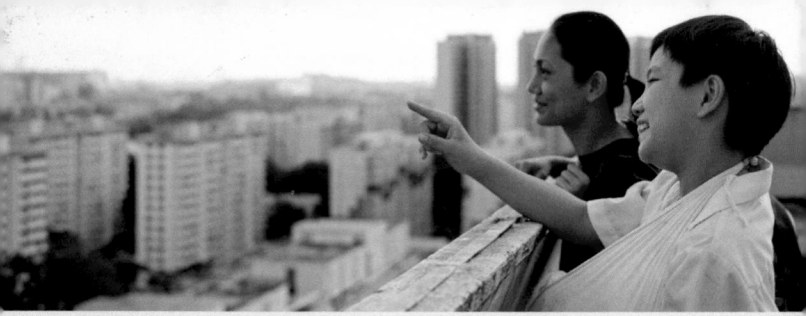

A shot from 'Ilo Ilo'

BOOKS AND FILM

Most of the Singapore's literary works portray and explore various aspects of society. Given the small domestic market, it cannot be said that local literature has a huge following. Yet that doesn't mean that Singaporean's aren't voracious readers. Major bookshops like Kinokuniya continue to see a healthy crowd. Like their outlook in life, Singaporeans' tastes in books are international.

Over the last few years, the leading non-fiction author has been Singapore's former Prime Minister Lee Kwan Yew. Considered the founder of modern Singapore, Lee has written two books, which sold out within days of release. Other well-known books include Goh Poh Seng's *If We Dream Too Long*, widely recognised as the first true Singaporean novel. Catherine Lim is Singapore's most widely read author – largely due to her first two books of short stories, *Little Ironies: Stories of Singapore* and *Or Else, the Lightning God and Other Stories*.

Singaporeans love going to the movies – which explains the glut of cineplexes across the island. They enjoy a good Hollywood blockbuster, so much so that some movies open here even before they do in the US. For the most part, Singaporean films are slowly but steadily winning critical and commercial success, both at home and abroad.

Singapore had its golden age of cinema in the 1950s and 1960s when it was home to two powerhouse movie studios, Cathay and Shaw Brothers. Following Singapore's separation from Malaysia in 1965, the film industry moved to Kuala Lumpur. The 1990s saw a revival for the film industry. Director Eric Khoo's *12 Storeys* (1997) was the first Singaporean film shown at the Cannes Film Festival. But it was local TV comic-turned-filmmaker Jack Neo's *Money No Enough* (1998) that really warmed Singaporeans to local filmmaking efforts. In 2013, *Ilo Ilo* premiered at the Cannes Film Festival as part of the Directors' Fortnight, and the film was the first Singaporean feature film to win the Camera d'Or award.

To celebrate Singapore's 50th anniversary in 2015, seven local top directors are coming together to make a film, an omnibus of seven short stories, to celebrate the country and its people. Led by Royston Tan, the other award-winning filmmakers involved are Eric Khoo, Jack Neo, Kelvin Tong, Tan Pin Pin, Boo Jun-feng and K. Rajagopal.

Books

Complete Notes from Singapore: The Omnibus Edition (Neil Humphreys)
A British humourist writes on Singapore's idiosyncracies.

Conversations with Lee Kuan Yew (Tom Plate)
This candid, one-on-one conversation

The critically acclaimed 'My Magic'

with the internationally respected political leader is startling and even humorous at times.

Lee Kuan Yew: Hard Truths to Keep Singapore Going (Han Fook Kwang, Zuraidah Ibrahim, Chua Mui Hoong, Lydia Lim, Ignatius Low, Rachel Lin, Robin Chan)

This tome compiled by local writers is based on 32 hours of interviews at the Istana with Singapore's influential former Prime Minister.

The New Mrs Lee's Cookbook Vol. 1 and 2 (Shermay Lee)

A delightful introduction to Peranakan cuisine and culture plus well thought-out recipes.

One Fierce Hour (Alfian Sa'at)

Highly charged poems about life in Singapore by this acclaimed poet and playwright.

The Shrimp People (Rex Shelley)

An evocative tale on Singapore's Eurasians that won the National Book Prize.

Shiok!: Exciting Tropical Asian Flavours (Terry Tan and Christopher Tan)

One of the best books on Singaporean cuisine, with well-written, tried and tested recipes.

Singapore: Architecture of a Global City (Robert Powell, Albert K.S. Lim and Li Lian Chee)

Focuses on the city's modern architecture and skyline.

Films

12 Storeys (1997)

Director Eric Khoo's indulgently lengthy frames capture the lives of lonely residents in a block of flats. The only Singaporean film to date to be selected for the Un Certain Regard section at Cannes.

15 (2002)

This film, directed by Royston Tan, about restless Chinese teenagers who turn to gangs was heavily censored on release (references to gangs are considered risky in Singapore). It's available uncut on DVD only in the UK and US.

Ah Boys To Men (2012–3)

Jack Neo's successful two-part film revolves around the lives of a group of recruits serving their National Service in Singapore. It is to date the highest-grossing Singaporean movie of all time.

Be With Me (2005)

Inspired by the life story of Theresa Chan, an elderly woman who has been deaf and blind since she was a teenager, this Eric Khoo film is made up of three poignant stories interwoven around the desire for love and companionship. It was the opening film for the Directors' Fortnight programme at Cannes in 2005.

My Magic (2008)

After the screening of My Magic at the 61st Cannes Film Festival, a 15-minute plus standing ovation ensued. The Eric Khoo film – a mostly Tamil drama about an alcoholic magician struggling to repair his relationship with his young son – was Singapore's first contender for the Palme d'Or.

ABOUT THIS BOOK

This *Explore Guide* has been produced by the editors of Insight Guides, whose books have set the standard for visual travel guides since 1970. With top-quality photography and authoritative recommendations, these guidebooks bring you the very best routes and itineraries in the world's most exciting destinations.

BEST ROUTES

The routes in the book provide something to suit all budgets, tastes and trip lengths. As well as covering the destination's many classic attractions, the itineraries track lesser-known sights, and there are also ex-cursions for those who want to extend their visit outside the city. The routes embrace a range of interests, so whether you are an art fan, a gourmet, a history buff or have kids to entertain, you will find an option to suit.

We recommend reading the whole of a route before setting out. This should help you to familiarise yourself with it and enable you to plan where to stop for refreshments – options are shown in the 'Food and Drink' box at the end of each tour.

For our pick of the tours by theme, consult Recommended Routes for… (see pages 4–5).

INTRODUCTION

The routes are set in context by this introductory section, giving an overview of the destination to set the scene, plus background information on food and drink, shopping and more, while a succinct history timeline highlights the key events over the centuries.

DIRECTORY

Also supporting the routes is a Directory chapter, with a clearly organised A–Z of practical information, our pick of where to stay while you are there and select restaurant listings; these eateries complement the more low-key cafés and restaurants that feature within the routes and are intended to offer a wider choice for evening dining. Also included here are some nightlife listings and our recommendations for books and films about the destination.

ABOUT THE AUTHOR

This new guide to Singapore was written by Malaysian-born journalist and writer Amy Van. Amy has lived in Singapore for more than 15 years and calls this city state her home. With more than a decade of editorial experience, she contributes to a variety of food, travel and lifestyle publications in the region as well as international travel guides. She has also worked on numerous book projects for Insight Guides, among others, as writer and editor.

CONTACT THE EDITORS

We hope you find this Explore Guide useful, interesting and a pleasure to read. If you have any questions or feedback on the text, pictures or maps, please do let us know. If you have noticed any errors or outdated facts, or have suggestions for places to include on the routes, we would be delighted to hear from you. Please drop us an email at insight@apaguide.co.uk. Thanks!

CREDITS

Explore Singapore
Contributors: Amy Van
Commissioning Editor: Sarah Clark
Pictures: Tom Smyth
Map Production: original cartography Berndtson & Berndtson, updated by Apa Cartography Department
Production: Rebeka Davies
Photo credits: 123RF 78, 124; Alamy 136, 137; Apa Publications 34, 35L, 36, 52, 62, 62/63, 63L, 64, 65, 66, 67, 68, 69, 70, 71, 73, 74, 75, 80, 82, 87, 89, 92, 93L, 118; Rory Daniel 100MR; Dreamstime 2ML, 2MC, 6MR, 8/9, 14/15, 16, 28MR, 85L, 118/119; Fairmont Hotels 102, 103; Fullerton Hotel 100MC; Getty Images 4MC, 26, 51, 54, 95, 97, 98, 98/99; IndoChine Group 110; iStock 5MR, 18, 19, 24, 24/25, 28/29T, 31, 32, 42/43, 44, 45L, 46/47, 55, 56, 56/57, 57L, 58/59, 61L, 76/77, 79, 80/81, 83, 84, 84/85, 86, 94; Leonardo 44/45, 60, 100/101T, 106, 107, 108, 116; Marina Bay Sands 4TL, 5T, 25L, 28ML, 104/105, 110/111, 111L, 112, 112/113, 113L; Marina Mandarin 100MC; National Museum of Singapore 39; Peranakan Museum 38; Photoshot 27; Raffles Hotel 28ML, 100MR, 100ML; Rasa Sentosa 100ML; Red Dot Design Museum 53; Shangri-La Hotel 6MC, 116/117; Singapore Art Museum 41; Singapore Tourism Board 1, 2MC, 2ML, 4ML, 5MR, 6MR, 6ML, 6/7T, 8L, 9, 14, 15L, 17, 20, 21, 22/23, 23L, 30, 34/35, 40, 60/61, 81L, 90, 114, 114/115, 122, 122/123, 123L, 125, 126; STB/Christopher White 128/129; STB/Joseph Goh Meng Huat 6ML; Swissotel Hotels & Resorts 2MR; The Arts House 33; Vincent Ng/Apa 2MR, 2/3T, 4BC, 5M, 6MC, 10, 11, 12, 13, 22, 28MC, 28MC, 28MR, 37, 48, 49, 72, 88, 91, 92/93, 96, 115L, 119L, 120/121, 127, 130, 131, 132/133, 134, 135; Wildlife Reserves Singapore 99L
Cover credits: coloured shutters, *Corbis*
Front Cover BL: skyline, *Dreamstime* **Back Cover:** (Left) Raffles statue, *Dreamstime* **(Right):** dragon *Singapore Tourism Board*

Printed by CTPS – China
© 2015 Apa Publications (UK) Ltd
All Rights Reserved

First Edition 2015

DISTRIBUTION

Worldwide
APA Publications GmbH & Co. Verlag KG (Singapore branch)
7030 Ang Mo Kio Ave 5, 08-65
Northstar @ AMK, Singapore 569880
Email: apasin@singnet.com.sg
UK and Ireland
Dorling Kindersley Ltd (a Penguin Company)
80 Strand, London, WC2R 0RL, UK
Email: sales@uk.dk.com
US
Ingram Publisher Services
One Ingram Blvd, PO Box 3006, La Vergne, TN 37086-1986
Email: ips@ingramcontent.com
Australia and New Zealand
Woodslane
10 Apollo St, Warriewood NSW 2102, Australia
Email: info@woodslane.com.au

INDEX

MAP LEGEND		
● Start of tour	★ Place of interest	▭ Park
→ Tour & route direction	❶ Tourist information	▭ Important building
❶ Recommended sight	⚊ Statue/monument	▭ Hotel
❷ Recommended restaurant/café	✉ Main post office	▭ Transport hub
	🚍 Main bus station	▭ Market/store
	◪ MRT station	▭ Pedestrian area
	♨ Viewpoint	▭ Urban area